G000089685

OF ROLLING WATERS AND ROARING WIND

A CELEBRATION OF THE WOMAN SONG

Edited by

LYNDA KATSUNO-ISHII

AND EDNA J. ORTEZA

WCC PUBLICATIONS, GENEVA

i

Layout and cover design: Marie Arnaud Snakkers

Music typeset by Terry MacArthur and Ulisses Mantovani

ISBN 2-8254-1287-2

© 2000 WCC Publications, World Council of Churches,
150 route de Ferney, 1211 Geneva 2, Switzerland
Web site: http://www.wcc-coe.org

Printed in Switzerland

Contents

FOREWORD:

WE WILL SING, WE WILL DANCE, WE WILL PRAY OUR NEW VISIONS!

Water was the central symbol at the Decade Festival held in Harare, Zimbabwe, in November 1998, just prior to the eighth assembly of the World Council of Churches. The Festival was a celebration to mark the end of the Ecumenical Decade – Churches in Solidarity with Women (1988-1998). As the Festival was being designed, it was decided that worship and Bible study should be central to the event. Each morning Lusmarina Campos Garcia, a pastor and liturgical dancer from Brazil, added a little more water to an earthenware pot containing water that women had carried from their own nations and regions – water collected at worship in end-of-Decade events in many places in the world. The water symbolized the tears, the joys, the hopes of women from all continents. The ecumenical liturgy prepared by a small team of women, the music, prayers and songs, celebrated women's love for and commitment to the church.

It was appropriate that the Ecumenical Decade should conclude in this way since it has over its ten years given space to many creative liturgical expressions. In liturgy and ritual women have again and again used symbols that express effectively their deepest aspirations and hopes for the church. They have used a language that carefully includes women's biblical history and faith experience, although traditional worship in most denominations has tended to exclude women in language and form. Whenever the story of the Decade is told, it will have to acknowledge the creativity and commitment with which women have developed worship and liturgical material, art work and graphics to give expression to an alternative theological vision. Women in different parts of the world, from different cultural contexts and from different ecclesial situations speak in their own language – sometimes a new language – to express their longing for a new community in Christ.

The worship life of Decade-related gatherings in all parts of the world has held these events together, giving them the environment for difficult, sometimes divisive, sometimes painful discussions. It has also provided the atmosphere for the celebrative aspects of these meetings. In the liturgy, says Gail Lynn Unterberger, "women's affinity for mystery, warmth, the earthy and concrete, the particular, listening, humour, storytelling, candour, availability and paradox provides a new prayer life from the point of view of women struggling to be free, bringing along their children, families, the earth and the cosmos" ("Preaching", in Letty M. Russell and J. Shannon Clarkson, eds, *Dictionary of Feminist Theologies*, Louisville, Westminster John Knox, 1996).

This book is a collection of prayers, meditations, poems, reflections from women all over the world – largely drawn from Decade-related resources. We are grateful to Lynda Katsuno-Ishii for kindly helping to put this book together, ably supported by Edna Orteza. They have collected the material, organized it into chapters and written a helpful introduction to the text. A reading of these texts will reveal the passion with which women express what they experience. Often it is only the written word which gives them a space to express what lies hidden deep within their hearts. We are grateful to all the writers for their contributions.

The eighth assembly of the World Council of Churches spoke of an "ecumenism of the heart", noting that "the foundation for all our ecumenical engagement is our response to God. It asks for nothing less than conversion of our hearts. Because ecumenism is directed towards God, and to the world so loved by God, worship and spirituality must take even deeper roots in the heart of all we do" (Diane Kessler, ed., *Together on the Way: Official Report of the Eighth Assembly of the WCC*, Geneva, WCC, 1999, p.143).

We as women bring to the ecumenical table our songs of praise, prayers and reflections which capture our dreams for a more inclusive church that will respond to such an ecumenical vision. We offer these our gifts, in the hope that our theological and spiritual visions will inspire a liturgical renewal movement within the ecumenical movement and in the church.

Aruna Gnanadason
Coordinator-Women/Justice, Peace and Creation Team

INTRODUCTION:

CALL TO CELEBRATION

I come from a small place called Miljevina, which is situated near Focce in eastern Bosnia. When we were forced into exile, I began writing poems. The poems are about the war in Bosnia and Herzegovina. War... killing... crying... dying... pain... war... These things hurt, and even though I am far from them it is as if I was there in their midst. That is the love for one's homeland, Bosnia; for the town of my birth, Focce; for the father who fights for freedom; for the mothers who cry; for the ones left behind; and for everything else. These wounds have driven me to write down my thoughts on all things. Here are the poems. I hope you will like them.

Poems, songs, prayers, stories, reflections, liturgies are means of communicating thoughts, ideas and emotions. Like Lajla Talovic, the 14-year-old refugee from Bosnia whose words are quoted above, women have often used poetry to articulate their innermost thoughts and feelings, their experiences of power and vulnerability, of struggle and hope, of courage and resistance, of longing and fulfilment. Poems, like symbols, move us beyond ourselves and express meanings deeper than everyday words.

The poems and reflections included here are about the longings of the woman-soul and of the woman-heart beating in rhythm with other woman beings. These are about the surging of the womb spirit in its anticipation of the birth of a new generation of women and men, a new way of being. With these, we invite you to participate in the celebration of the spiritual gifts of the Ecumenical Decade – Churches in Solidarity with Women. To provide a framework for reflection, they have been organized under headings derived from the poems themselves.

WOMB SPIRIT

"Womb Spirit" by Lynda Katsuno-Ishii traces the seeds of a new vision in the ecumenical movement, the Decade. Using feminine images – expectation, anticipation, growing, sustaining, the breaking of the waters, birthing, entering a new space, taking the breath of the Spirit, receiving new life – it reflects on the different phases of the Decade and expresses the hopes of women beyond the Decade. The allusion to the womb reminds us of the birthing, caring, nurturing qualities of women.

WOMAN SONG

This section on self-identity and self-affirmation reflects the relational character of women's self-identification. As women struggle for identity, they do not separate themselves from the realities surrounding their lives, including their oneness with the earth. The self-revelation alludes to social norms and values which society has imposed on women – expectations and gender traps which keep them in subordinate positions wherever they find themselves. There are images of wars and fighters who must seek the safety and solitude of the mountains; of being strangers in a foreign land; of having to work each day at the risk of their children growing up without knowing them; of women being sacrificed for dowry and as victims of male lust; of the collective abuse of Dalit women; of poverty and of having to take turns to eat; of servanthood, back-breaking hours of work and abuse; of finally knowing what the body had long known; of women waiting, hoping, sharing. Judith Sequeira speaks of the "rainbow-coloured cross" she will carry on the road to liberation.

WOMAN, WHY ARE YOU WEEPING?

Irja Askola's poem "Woman, why are you weeping?" brings us back to the tomb of the resurrection. It speaks of hurt souls and beaten bodies, of bruises and bleeding wounds, of destroyed dreams and suffocated beginnings, of lonely lips and rejected wombs. It is at the same time an invitation to meet in the garden of the empty tomb, to celebrate, to dance. The other poems reveal intense emotions – Savitri's unbearable agony, pressured to kill her own child, a daughter; fear of the violence on city streets at night; sadness over the loss of dreams for children and grandchildren; longing for sacred space; anxiety over the degradation of the environment; anger that young women are forced to lose their virginity in order to survive; the pain of having to respond to children's questions about killer birds, death and destruction, when there are simply no answers; the longing for solidarity.

WOMEN, WHY ARE WE STILL WEEPING?

Continuing the thread of Irja Askola's poem, Lajla Talovic raises questions about the fundamental values of peace, freedom, love, happiness. *When the sun rises, the cold rain leaves and the dove of peace comes, is that freedom?* There is pain over lives wasted in wars, and concern about Aboriginal women having to bear the burden of history. *How long must we wait? How are we to be women clothed with the sun? What does God require of us? How can we sing a new song?* The questions are at the same time expressions of solidarity, which show how individual pain becomes collective suffering for women.

THE JUSTICE OF WOMEN'S LIBERATION

If you deny liberation to women, there is no more life in this world. The *one* story can only unfold in community with men. This section includes poems, stories and reflections by men, expressions of solidarity with women which come from a recognition of the wrongs of history, a profound understanding of the human responsibility to change pervading values and perspectives, and an affirmation of the courageous life-giving struggles of women.

THE GOSPEL ACCORDING TO YOU

What motivates women to continue with their struggle? In the experience of women, education and consciousness-raising, telling their own stories, analyzing and reflecting on the common story, expressions of solidarity, and actual engagement in various issues and concerns have fostered deeper understanding and stronger commitment to change. An important dimension is faith. While scholars had long neglected the important role of women in biblical history, women in theology have contributed greatly by challenging the dominant interpretation of the scriptures. Women in the churches began reading with new eyes and found themselves in the heart of the biblical message, opening up enormous possibilities for a reconstruction of the woman story.

> New theological visions are being born out of the womb of women's experiences of suffering, pain and struggles..., drawing strength from the intuitive, the poetic, the lyrical. Women all over the world recognize that traditional expectations of long suffering and sacrifice... can no longer be accepted. Women affirm theologies of hope and action, of laughter and joy, of liberation and freedom for all God's people and creation ... (From **Women's Visions**, edited by Ofelia Ortega, WCC, 1995).

In this section are poems about new images of God – God listening in unexpected places, refusing to conform to imposed norms, waiting, teaching, dancing; about a vision of Christ coming, celebrating small victories with women, weeping tears of pain, singing a song of liberation, dancing the dance of freedom. Stories of Joanna and Rizpah, St Nina and St Brigit, and those who saw the star provide the inspiration to nurture the hope. An underlying theme is the assurance that God continues to weave the tapestry of a new creation.

THE SONG OF PEACE

The retelling of the woman story begins here with Mary Southard's "Song of Peace", a celebration of the woman song. There are affirmations of the gifts and work of women – a recollection of sleepless nights and endless agonies, but also of hopes and dreams, of innovation and creativity, of how women make things grow, humming to themselves but hearing the tune of others. There are also images of the justice tree blooming, of each bird bringing twigs to make together a new nest, of regaining *we*-ness, of throwing stones in a calm lake to create ripples of life, of women leaping and dancing to songs that belong to them. These are songs of life, speaking profoundly about the life-affirming nature of women.

MAGDALENE DANCING IN CRIMSON

Here are more resources to help in the celebration, beginning with Yuko Yuasa's short play about the woman who had followed Jesus to the cross, who waited in the garden, who witnessed the resurrection, and who now dances and tells us of eternal love. Included are praises and prayers on various concerns of women – their fears and longings, sisters in the struggle, indigenous women, countries in crisis, the earth – as well as suggestions for a liturgy on the table of life, prepared by Cora Tabing-Reyes.

HOLY WEEK MEDITATIONS

At the Ecumenical Centre in Geneva, the Decade, launched at Easter 1988, concluded with meditations during Holy Week 1998. Reflections from Monday to Thursday revolved around events surrounding the passion and death of Jesus. Of particular significance are how these events were remembered – with sounds, movement, the use of symbols and images, and the exploration of the various possibilities for using cloth in worship.

SONGS

Songs, put together by Terry MacArthur and Ulisses Mantovani, are included here to further enhance the celebration. The songs have been carefully selected to represent the richness of tone, rhythm and language present in many cultures as well as the shared longing for a world community. Note that some of the songs were written by men.

THE CELEBRATION CONTINUES...

The celebration does not end with the use of these resources. You can open up spaces for such a process to take place wherever and whenever possible. The celebration continues for as long as women nurture the hope and the creativity, the courage and the determination towards a reconstruction of the *one* story.

Let us open our hearts to receive these offerings, and accept the challenges they bring to us.

WOMB SPIRIT

WOMB SPIRIT

seeds of a new vision are planted...
Nairobi 1985
the United Nations Decade for Women
comes to an end with a grand global celebration
I am transformed
Women of the World Council of Churches and many others
know the work cannot stop now
We have a vision for a new time, a new space

expectation...
our work and our plans are greeted with enthusiasm by many
yet, strains of "Ten years – too long! One year should be enough!"
are heard in the halls
but we are determined
and will not give up our dreams, our goals for the journey
to create this new space and time

anticipation...
our plans and work become reality
as churches around the world join together at Easter 1988
to begin an Ecumenical Decade – Churches in Solidarity with Women
this part of the dream and the vision becomes incarnate
we have begun to roll away the stone

growing...
you – seeds of new visions and dreams!
you are growing in the space of this womb time
solidarity is growing
we see the seeds of justice
taking root in places where the soil was barren and dry
and courage is growing!
I spend a summer working with favela women in Rio de Janeiro
they are turning their pain into action
they are following the trails of tears of their disappeared children
"all we want is our children back, even if it's just their bones..."

sustaining...
the spirit of women who have gone before us
sustains us throughout the journey
women who were known throughout the world
women who will forever remain nameless
our courage is sustained by their faith and determination
by the lives they have given
and all that we do we do in memory of them
and my own life is sustained and nurtured by
Mary, Anthony, Richard, Teruko, Dorothy, Chiaki, Ise

the breaking of the waters...
I am transformed by the women around the world
with whom I have worked
their passion and drive to create and re-create the world
is like the mysterious energy
that causes the breaking of the water within womb
sometimes this breaking of water to bring new life
was through a woman giving her life
her blood mingled with water gave life to others

birthing...
we begin to see new birth
new life experiences being formed and taking shape
after thirty years of bloody civil war
a sister in Angola tells us that she is finally learning
the traditional weaving of her people
her woven basket sits before me – empty, yet full of courage and hope
a space now being filled with strength and new life
and a new story is being woven...

a new space...
giving birth means transformation
means going from womb and entering a new space
in his relationship with all the people and with women in particular
Jesus shows us his radical vision for a new community
dare we hope that we too have created new communities
based on new models of relationships of justice and love
the journey does not stop now
for we still search for that shalom – right relationships
with each other, with God and with all of creation

the breath of life...
what will happen in this time following the Ecumenical Decade
in a new time and space
the new born Body created from the passion, commitment and work
of the past ten years
takes its breath of the Holy Spirit
and we are filled with power and courage and renewed energy
seeds for still other dreams and visions are planted anew
and a new Womb Spirit begins to flow through our lives

Lynda Katsuno-Ishii, Canada

WOMAN SONG

I COME FROM THE EARTH

I come from the Earth,
I am the child of the Earth
The source of my life
Where my placenta is buried.
My connection is made
Source of my life.

Marie Ropeti, Samoa

I COME FROM THE LAND OF SPIRITS

I come from Korea, the land of spirits full of *Han*. *Han* is anger. *Han* is resentment. *Han* is bitterness. *Han* is grief. *Han* is broken-heartedness and the raw energy for the struggle for liberation. In my tradition, people who were killed or died unjustly became wandering spirits, the *Han*-ridden spirits. They are all over the place seeking the chance to make the wrong right. Therefore the living people's responsibility is to listen to the voices of the *Han*-ridden spirits and to participate in the spirits' work of making right whatever is wrong.

These *Han*-ridden spirits in our people's history have been agents through whom the Holy Spirit has spoken her compassion and wisdom for life. Without hearing the cries of these spirits, we cannot hear the voice of the Holy Spirit... They are the icons of the Holy Spirit who became tangible and visible to us. Because of them we can feel, touch and taste the concrete bodily historical presence of the Holy Spirit in our midst...

After many years of infantile prayers, I know there is no magic solution to human sinfulness and for healing our wounds. I also know that I no longer believe in an omnipotent, macho, warrior God who rescues all good guys and punishes all bad guys. Rather, I rely on the compassionate God who weeps with us for life in the midst of the cruel destruction of life.

Chung Hyun-Kyung, Korea

QUIET THOUGHTS

I am a woman
Of hidden thoughts and stifled feelings
Expressing myself
In the children I breed
And the garden I nurture

I am a woman
Of tired dreams and wishful aspirations

Taming the future
In the *umu* fires lit
And the final chores before sleep

I am a woman
Of humble horizons and vivid perspectives
Budgeting the costs
In family obligations
And food for the evening table

I am a woman
of sad expectations and pre-determined roads
Resigning to life
In children grown and gone
And morning chores at dawn

But I am a woman
Of quiet resilience and persistent patience
Sharing my endurance
In the progress of island nations
And the leaders I made.

Vaine Rasmussen, Cook Islands

WHO AM I?

When I was born
Everyone present was eager to know.
"Congratulations,"
They said to my mother.
"What sex is the baby?",
They enquired.
"A girl,"
Mother said in reply.

People came from near and far.
Gifts they presented of various types,
Labels I was given:
A future daughter-in-law
A wife, for the old man
A grandmother, for some
An aunt to my brother's children
The list was endless.

Many qualities I was given.
Cleverness was a virtue given
Because of my blue eyes.
Beautiful, as it was said I took
After my mother.
So soon I wondered
A bright girl I was told
The reason I did not know.

A good woman worth marrying,
I was told, but why
I did not know.
A nurse was said to be my profession.
An industrious future mother I was labelled,
Sweeping the house,
Washing and ironing clothes
Was a speciality.
As for cooking,
I was an expert
Because my mother gave me
The relevant training
To be a woman of tomorrow.

Playing with boys
I was not allowed.
My brothers were to be
Given the respect as if
They were my father.
Their laundry and meals
I had to prepare
Because they were men
And I was a *woman*.

But why do I have
To do extra work just because
I was born a girl child?
Did I ever have
The opportunity to choose to be a girl?
What did the boy child do
To deserve the best treatment?
Can someone please tell me
The secret behind all this favouritism?

They call me *wo-man*
My brother is *man*.
This implies that I am
A man plus.
Perhaps that is why I am suffering:
For being more than a man.

Elizabeth Mamhene, Zimbabwe

WHO AM I?

I was ignored by men.
I was regarded as
a child-bearer
a pig-raiser
and a house-keeper.
I stayed at home
and nursed the kids,
I cleaned the house
and fed the pigs.
I wanted freedom
and looked for it
but was beaten
and sent home.

I want love and equality.
I want justice among men,
women and children.

Education has come to my country,
Independence has come to my country.
Has freedom come to my country?

I am the mother of the nation,
I am the producer of life,
I build Vanuatu.
Has equality come to my country?

Dorah Obed, Vanuatu

I AM A PROCESS

I am a process
I am going on...
I know that I am more than what I am now.

I gave birth to my children
I soared to the sky with my belly up
Wonder of wonders
I am a mother!

I am a woman
I feel free
Like a bird soaring through the summer winds.

But alas, I forgot...
For as long as one sister
Is oppressed, battered, dehumanized
I am not free!

I am connected...
through our indigenous cultures
through our ancestors
To all our relations.

I am moving on
carrying everyone's
aspirations, dreams and visions...

I am connected.

Violeta Marasigan, USA

TRIBESWOMAN

I stand and wait
Quietly in the doorway
And my heart throbs
With pride, my belly
Swells with love.
I drink the satisfaction
In the eyes of my husband
And children as they eat
The vegetables I planted
The fruits I reaped
The rice I cooked.

See the muscles
Rippling in my husband's
Arms and thighs,
Bronzed by the sun
Moist from the rain and
Dewdrops in the fields.
See my children's
Limbs as tender
As the bamboo shoots
Painfully growing
To meet the stars
And till the land.

Yes, they need food
As they say
More than I do
Since I only stay
At home, grow
Camote, wash
Clothes, clean
The hut, bear
Babies for more
peasant hands
From dawn to sunup
Sunup to dawn.

I swallow my saliva,
Am deaf to my gurgling
Stomach, I stand
And wait for my toes
To fetch water
To fill the bowl
Of soup, and serve
Strangers, too.
My frail frame
Recedes, quivering
between the wind
And the vanishing food.

My body contains
The dream of my father
Sweat of my husband
Hope of my children...
But
Could it be possible
It is wrong
To stand and wait
Like this –
A heap of ribs,
A forsaken idol –
As my foremothers did before me
many moons ago
In the shadow of the mountains?
Could it be possible
It is wrong?
Could it be
Possible?

Maria Pl. Lanot, Philippines

TODAY IS MY TURN TO EAT

Today, it is my turn to have some food.
Yesterday my two brothers and my sisters ate.
They were luckier than I was:
Daddy did not come home.
He stayed overnight at the home of our other mother.
Our group: that is me, Mummy and my sister Jeanne and little Junior.
Junior has something to eat every day:
some cassava porridge, because he is still a baby.
At school, during the break, the girls used to share their fritters
with me.
But school is no longer for me;
Daddy has said there was not enough money left to pay for all of us.
Only my brothers still go to school;
for us girls, we were told that we will find husbands.

I shall perhaps attend literacy classes with the other Mummies, as
they are free of charge.
I shall perhaps go with my cousin and do some trade in the market
place.
I shall perhaps go to town and do some babysitting for the white
people.
But Mummy told us tomorrow she would go and get some maize
from Grand-Dad's fields in our village.
She will be back next week,
She will sell the maize and buy medicine for Jeanne's malaria.
I will stay, to carry Junior on my back and prepare his cassava
porridge every day.
It is good he is not so heavy, and this is my chance:
I can have some of his porridge!
I feel like asking Daddy why they want to put us out of our home;
I feel like asking Daddy why he wants to sell our transistor;
I feel like telling Daddy that I have outgrown my dress,
that it is all worn out, that my shoes are too small.
But Daddy only comes home to change his clothes.
And he is always cross.

Dear God, why do we have to suffer this way?

Group reflection from an All Africa Conferences of Churches
consultation on "The Theological Basis for Child Survival and
Development", Porto-Novo, Benin

HE IS THE MAN

I leave him in the blanket at early dawn
Warm, wrapped up and asleep,
As I go to sweep his mother's yard
And put warm water for his father's bath.
He is the man.

I serve him first
Ugali, two drumsticks,
The other meat goes to the others.
I call the children for the remaining soup.
I can stay without.
He is the man.

He leaves for the township beer-hall.
I remain behind – cooking, cleaning,
Washing, bathing the children,
Sweeping, sewing, weeding,
Spreading the bed he had just left.
He is the man.

My back is tired, sore, painful.
It is dark.
The crying child has just fallen asleep.
He returns from the beer-hall
Reeking of sweat and alcohol.
He climbs on worn-out me;
It is his turn now.
He is the man.

When is my turn?

Fridah Muyale, Zimbabwe

WORKING MOTHER

My children don't know me:
They call me Jully
not Mummy.
They see me
Two hours before bedtime,
An hour in the mornings.
No time for a cuddle, or play;
No time to feed, bathe or clothe them –
Just a peck on the cheek and
"Bye bye, be good!
See you at four."
I'm never home during the week –
Too busy making money.
The only times I see them
They are asleep in bed.
I spend the nights alone
With the house-girl.
My children don't know me.

Jully Sipolo, Solomon Islands

DON'T CALL ME A STRANGER

Don't call me a stranger:
the language I speak sounds different,
but the feelings it expresses are the same.

Don't call me a stranger:
I need to communicate,
Especially when language is not understood.

Don't call me a stranger:
I need to be together
Especially when loneliness cools my heart.

Don't call me a stranger:
I need to feel at home,
Especially when mine is very
far away from yours.

Don't call me a stranger:
I need a family,
because mine I've left to work for yours.

Don't call me a stranger:
The soil we step on is the same
but mine is not "the promised land".

Don't call me a stranger:
the colour of my passport is different,
but the colour of our blood is the same.

Don't call me a stranger:
I toil and struggle in your land,
and the sweat of our brows is the same.

Don't call me a stranger:
borders, we created them,
and the separation that results is the same.

Don't call me a stranger:
I am just your friend,
but you do not know me yet.

Don't call me a stranger:
we cry for justice and peace in different ways,
but our God is the same.

Don't call me a stranger:
yes, I am a migrant,
but our God is the same.

Author Unknown, Philippines

DOWRY DEATHS

I'm Manjushree,
Currently making your acquaintance
Through front page headlines,
But have I really succeeded in communicating with you?
That only the police and reporters have been doing
And you have been deriving your opinions from their reports.
But today I want to speak to you.

I'm a Shaila suffocated to death in flames –
I'm a Chanda sacrificed for dowry –
I'm a Mathura, victim of male lust –
I'm a Draupadi, property of five men –
I'm a representative of numerous, nameless, oppressed women –
I'm Manjushree
I have no caste, no religion, no class, no age.

Actually speaking
I ought to have spoken long ago,
When Draupadi was gambled away by her husbands
When she was disrobed in public...
But I viewed her suffering as just another "story".

When Maya and Mathura fell victim to police atrocities,
I said to myself, "How am I concerned with the police?
I, who am so educated, cultured, etc."
So many news items on rape, molestation appeared,
I turned up my nose and said,
"The girl must be of loose character."
"Collective abuse on Dalit women," read the headlines.
Discussion at home: "Probably some stunt
by the opposition and 'news' for the papers."

When Saila Latkar's case came to light
I was deeply touched,
But I did not even dream that "my people"
would be so cruel and decadent.
This male-dominated culture
with its religious and social traditions
was in reality a monstrous python
which had me in its grip,
but this I did not realize.
I maintained aloof
because of my virtue, my modesty,
my "good breeding",
my middle-class culture,
I remained mute – and lonely.

But today –
I'm one with all these suffering women
and because of my identification with them
I can speak out openly.

Today there are loud speeches
Lamenting my death;
Today processions of protest
are being made in my behalf;
Newspapers fill their columns with news of me.

Now – who is to blame in this matter?
Are we women to be blamed?
Or our parents and relatives
who handed us this culture of silent suffering?
Or society which forces our parents and others
to abide by the rules of this culture
which has handicapped us since our very birth?
Not only that, but taught us to glorify the concept
that a woman should always be dependent on a man.

They may bring down the law upon the culprits.
A few culprits may be set free
by clever arguments by their clever advocates,
But why is it that the goddess of justice
is always blind(folded).
But aren't you all keeping your eyes open?
Aren't you listening to what I am saying?
I am eagerly and anxiously awaiting your reply.
I – Manjushree.

Author Unknown, India

DO I FEEL MYSELF LIKE GOD'S IMAGE?

Do I feel myself like God's image? Am I made in the image of God? Are you crazy? How can you ask me such a thing?

How can a prostitute be like God? Do you mean by your question: am I like a portrait of God? As if God, looking at me, could see himself? No, you are crazy!

Don't even think about it. It's a sin even to think about such a thing!

I want God as something beautiful, clean, pure and very strong; to help me and to help others. I don't want God to be like me. I don't want to be an image of God. Imagine. If that was so, no one would believe in God anymore. And the world would be crazy. The night wouldn't follow the day and the stars wouldn't lie together with the moon.

Maybe, looking into my heart, people can find good things. It's the place where I keep pureness, beauty, dreams and, very deep in my heart, maybe I can find a little piece of God.

But there is another thing I remember. God is powerful. Nobody gives orders to God. And I think that, in this case, I am a little like God; nobody gives me orders. That's a joke, so don't worry.

When I got pregnant I didn't know if I should have the baby. Everybody gave me advice; there were many opinions. But I had the baby. It was a boy. The birth of my son was such a marvellous sensation. And I asked myself: doesn't God make us too? Aren't we God's sons and daughters?

I don't know if God loves us as much as I love my son.

And I have also learned that God can forgive us everything. Everything can be forgiven. My son does not know I am a prostitute. I think he would not accept it. But a mother accepts everything from her son. Do you think God is like a mother? That God really does forgive everything the sons and daughters do wrong?

I really believe in God. But I really don't know if God is in me, maybe a little bit.

The church says that everybody is God's sons and daughters. But why, when I go to church, am I ashamed? I look everywhere to see if someone can imagine I am a prostitute.

Why do I go into church with my head down? If God knows me why am I ashamed when it's his house?

But I talk to God. And I ask him to help me to be happy. I just need a few things, a little house, a little garden and to love my son.

Davina Moscoso, Brazil

I WORE THE SILKEN GOWN OF THE EMPRESS

I wore the silken gown of the Empress
And felt the squiggle of worms
As they spat out the silken threads
From mouths that cannot speak.

I wore the silken gown of the Empress
And felt the pinch of fingers
Of peasant girls plucked from mothers' arms
By takers of energies.

I wore the silken gown of the Empress
And felt the heat of bosoms
Of workers getting milked
By takers of energies.

I wore the silken gown of the Empress
and felt the strength of fists
Of people finding out at last
That silken gowns are theirs.

Alma Fernandez, Philippines

I NEVER WAS A MAIDEN

behind me stands a long line of warriors
women so many, and men
fighters who defied relocation, extermination
seeking mountains, their safety and solitude
calling to me on the wind
that they have given to me for breath
carry us forward into the future, do not forget us
we have saved this day for you
the wind is singing never forget the battles
won and lost
never forget the sorrow behind the smiles that remain
let the day be shining again
and our memory of war fade
as our blood has faded
on the walls, on the trees
from the north to south, east to west
and south again
in this day of superjets
secret wars and ignorance
mission impossible challenges
the wind

Author Unknown

I NO LONGER SPOKE OF FREEDOM

I agreed
to let myself seek freedom
to find time away from pots and pans
to kill this urge in me to be sacrificial
to look for space, to laugh and look ahead.

And they agreed
to let me train against their indomitable wall.

I broke the rigid bonds that bound me
the rules which viciously roomed me in
the promises which made me obey
the taboos which made me subhuman.

But they broke
my spirit, scotched it even as it rose high.

I cried out
at the pain of the inauspicious widow
at the pangs of the childless woman
at the questions of the girl in the shadow
at the bitter, bitter pain of the raped.

Then they cried out
wanting to quell, to cloud, my newly found identity.

And I stopped, turned, no longer spoke of freedom.

Shiranee Mills, Sri Lanka

LET US CHOOSE LIFE

I am from occupied Palestine. As Palestinian women, we are struggling on two fronts: liberation on the national level, and liberation on the social level – liberation for women. We live daily in the midst of violence, and as victims of violence. We have a burning sense of injustice in response to the occupation by Israel of our homeland. Death is on every side. What do we do? Do we submit? Do we collaborate with injustice?

Are we captivated by our pain and suffering and bent down by our grief? No, we open our empty hands to God so they will be filled, empowered by God's love, peace and consolation turning our suffering into the joy of God's presence. God promised it and God will do it, if our hands remain open.

Women of Palestine are referred to as the glue of our society. We are the ones holding together our families while our husbands, brothers and sons are in prison, deported, wounded or killed. Many of us go to prison ourselves. We look after the fields, the animals, the home industries, the cooperatives, the children and the wounded. We work hard to see that our spirits are not broken by our bodies' pain. We continue to be a part of a mostly nonviolent struggle. We continue to work for a new dawn. We offer respect and concern on the one hand and defiance and non-cooperation with injustice on the other. We rage against, yet refuse to destroy or give in to hate and despair. This is our true revolution, not just a shuffle of death-wielding power.

We Palestinians and Middle-Easterners have been bleeding. The blood of our people is warm and the cries of anguish fill the air; but unfortunately, those who waged the war think that they can morally justify it. Daily we are reminded of life and death, and of the crucifixion. We feel the words of Jesus, who said, "Do not weep for me but for yourselves and your children." We often pray as Jesus did, so that the bitter cup may be taken away. We often shout with a loud voice, *"God, why have you forsaken us?"* We often ask ourselves if this is the purpose of God in our world. To use indiscriminately massive destructive weapons? To abuse energy resources and bring irreparable ecological damage? To use resources for military purposes and cause hunger, poverty and misery around the world?

We know that we are all created in the image of God and that our value comes from this likeness, but we definitely are not treated as such. Equality is the only humanizing element that brings people together without oppression or powerlessness, inferiority or superiority, and leaves no room for a double-standard morality and judgment.

As I speak to you today, I cannot be certain that my children and grandchildren are safe, or that I shall be able to return to my home. However, these worries will not make me less determined to work for justice.

Now, let us then choose life, work for peace and affirm the presence of the Holy Spirit by which our lives may be made more whole, more creative, more harmonious as we draw directly upon the power around us, within us and within all life.

Jean Zaru, Palestine

A WOMAN'S HANDS

I sit in a pew
Waiting. The Human
Becomes Divine.
The bread...
Perhaps kneaded by a woman's hands.
The wine...
Perhaps women worked in the winery.
But when the Human becomes
Divine
a woman's hands are taboo!
The Divine became human,
Penetrated a woman's womb
(Patriarchy had no place!).
Like soft petals unfolding
a crystal dewdrop.
The seed nestled
in a female form.
"You shall touch the Divine!"
The battered body
taken off the cross...
Women's hands gently
perform burial rites.
The crimson blood
must surely stain those hands.
Women's hands
caring hands.
"You shall touch the Divine!"
Even knead the bread
And share the wine.
I sit in a pew
Waiting
Hoping
Sharing.

Ranjini Rebera, Sri Lanka/Australia

My Cross

My cross is a rainbow-coloured cross,
Violet, Indigo, Blue, Green, Yellow, Orange, Red,
Colours of the rainbow,
A rainbow showed two centuries ago to Noah
in a promise never to destroy life again
in a promise fulfilled two thousand years ago.
Redeeming humankind
On the cross.

My cross is a rainbow-coloured cross
to liberate all,
North and South, East and West,
Black and White, Yellow and Brown.
Male and Female.

My cross is a rainbow coloured cross,
For I am blue with the pain of oppression
and blue with the struggle for freedom
and green with hope.

As I walk the royal (violet) road of liberation
with flowers yellow, orange and red,
Springing up in celebration
Of new life
Creating a new spring,
Of eternal liberation
in the resurrection of Christ.

Judith Sequeira, India

Woman, Why Are You Weeping?

WOMAN, WHY ARE YOU WEEPING?
(John 20:15)

There is a church
There will be many more
    Which moves from the Cross
    To the empty Tomb
    Carrying on its agenda
    The question
    "Woman, why are you weeping?"

And after having asked
Dares to listen
    Hurt souls, beaten bodies
    Bruised and bleeding wounds
    Cries after what she once had
    or never had

There is a church
There will be many more
    Which stays nearby the empty tomb
    And keeps asking
    Not being afraid of her tears
    "Woman, why are you weeping?"

And creates a space for her answers
    Destroyed dreams, suffocated beginnings
        Lonely lips, rejected wombs
    Unseen pain, unheard sighs
        Facts never recognized

There is a church
There will be many more
    Which continues the story
    Of the resurrected
    Acknowledging his first question
    After his burial
    "Woman, why are you weeping?"

And calls women
to remember
    To feel our whole journey
        Rather than, "Why don't you forget?"
        Or "Just Forgive"
    Which stops seeing us as victims
        Rather than those
        who survived
        And finally

We meet in the garden of the empty tomb
    All those coming from the shadow
    No more ashamed
    All of a sudden visible, beautiful
    Blooming colours

Invited for the celebration
    Of those
    Who remember

And we dance together as the church
    Following the example of the resurrected
    Asking his question
    Over and over again
    "Woman, why are you weeping?"

Irja Askola, Finland

MY CHILD

My child, whether you are alive or dead,
I am in agony.
When I think of the taunts you have to suffer
from your in-laws for dowry,
I feel it is better that you die now.
But as your mother
I am squeezed at my heart to see you die.
Forgive me.

Savitri, India,
a 23-year-old mother,
who uttered her unbearable agony
when she was pressured to kill her female baby

IMAGES OF RIO

Night...
It is night right now.
The shadows bring with them
A frightening beat,
A tense rhythm,
A silent memory.
Emptiness...
It is movement that is searched for.

Some rest,
Some fright.

In my neighbourhood,
Sounds insist to be heard.
A bomb,
Machine gun fire,
A rifle shot.
Then a scream,
A groan,
Then hours of agony.

Is it time to sleep?

He sat on a stone by the road leading to a *favela* (slum) in Santa Teresa. No one could see him, but he could see everyone who passed by or anyone who got closer.

I was looking for stones, dry leaves and branches to use for our worship. Suddenly I heard, "Stop! What are you doing here?"

I looked up and I saw a young boy, about twelve years old, pointing a rifle at me.

I explained to him what I was doing there. Then, with his feet, he drew an imaginary line on the ground and said, "Don't cross this line!"

The boy was an *olheiro*, someone who watches everything, everybody, every movement... and gives information to the drug traffickers. The boy was there to guard their borders.

He was looking at me. After a while he withdrew his rifle and rested it on the ground. Then he said, "Get out of here!"

Luzmarina Campos-Garcia, Brazil

WHERE CAN I GO?

Where can I go to find my sacred space?
Everywhere I go I am put here, there,
because I have no control.

Aha, food, glorious food...
Can I find an expression of my spirituality in my cooking
in my home?
Yes, this is my sacred space.
Sometimes I eat the leftovers,
as long as I have my sacred space.

I want to dance,
but I am told I'm too sensuous, I'm too fat.
Again I am controlled by a man's thoughts
and uncontrolled desires.

I commune with God in all things.
I go to church and I look for God in the small glasses of wine
and I see nothing,
but I share in one bowl of rice with my friends
and there I see God alive in the people around me.

I laugh, I cry, I eat from a banquet,
I nibble on a little biscuit.
Maybe God is in the fullness and in this emptiness too.
God, you are there in my isolation,
my desolation.

God, you are many, you are woman.
I am woman not because I can give birth,
or cook or clean.
I am woman because I am created
in your image

I know that when I suffer,
You suffer.
When I laugh,
You laugh
Yes
God, you are all around me.

Fei Taule'ale'ausumai, Aotearoa New Zealand

MIGRANT

Stranger in your homeland and stranger
amongst strangers
month after month you labour and everyday
is the same as yesterday.
But for you also there comes
the happier of days
That in which you return home:
and once you are home
the misunderstandings begin.
Your children have grown.
Of you, all they know is your name
but your affection, your love is enough
to draw them all to your heart
and the old tie is remade.
Your dreamed-of days
have vanished quickly
you go – and the old round begins.
Your soul once again you leave her
and alone, with your bag
filled with memories you go:
This is your whole life consumed
between an arrival and a departure
and to think that you went
to stay for only a year or two.

Rosa Coppola, Philippines

PAIN

Sing to us, Mama...

Mama, where are these killer birds from?

From far away, my love.

Mama, why do they come so many times?

They want to kill all of us, perhaps.

Why Mama?

I don't know, love; they are at war with us.

But they've killed Grandpa and Grandma and my friends
    and the cats, the flowers and the trees... they've done nothing
    wrong...

*I know my love, they were killed, but not because they've done
    anything wrong...*

Then why, why, why, Mama?

Simply because they were here.

Mama, I am sick, hungry and thirsty...

Yes, love, I know. We are all sick, hungry and thirsty.

*They have destroyed our water, our food, our baby milk powder,
    our hospitals and clinics, our doctors and nurses...*

They have also destroyed my school, Mama.

*Yes, love, and our mosque, our house and Tom's church... their
    thunder and lightning have covered up the sun with smoke, noise
    and blood... and fire and fury...*

Can't we go away from this heap of bricks, Mama?

*No, love, the roads are blocked by debris and rubble
    and they have destroyed the buses, taxis and lorries.*

Mama, where is Papa?

He has gone to fight the killer birds.

Will he come back to us soon, Mama?

I don't know. I hope so. Be a brave girl.

I miss Papa, Mama.

*Yes, I know, I miss him too. Now, be a good girl,
    give some water to baby brother, for my breasts are dry.*

Mama, Mama, the killer birds are roaring in again!

Be brave, my love, be brave...

Mama, Mama, the giant firecrackers are here!

They are giant bombs and rockets.

They are coming, Mama! They are exploding!

Be brave, be brave, my little girl.

Mama, I'm scared.

    *Lovely, take your baby brother to a safer place after the killer
    birds have flown away.*

And you, Mama? What about you? I'm scared, Mama.

Mama! Mama! Mama! Don't die, Mama! Don't leave us alone, Mama!

Sing to us, Mama, so that we may cry together.

    Mama! Mama! Mama! Mama!

Fan Yew Teng, Malaysia

WOMAN WITHOUT A NAME

Woman
without a name,
raped and abused
until break of day
then taken limb by limb
through the length of the land.
What symbolism is this?
What do I hear
in your silences?

Who questions your abuse
and the crime
against female sexuality
when the only question is misuse
of man's property?

Can I stand in solidarity
with your pain
and let the silence be
wordless?

Is your silence
louder than the cry
from the cross?

Kathy Galloway, Scotland

WHERE DO WE GO?

Where do we go
You and I
You and I

Help me sisters
To listen to you
Your cries from the deepest
agony you suffer

Help me hear your sighs and cries
Many nights sleepless
Alone, alone
Your heart beating in loneliness

Life's journey
Is too tough
My sisters and daughters
I also suffered many nights

Pain of growing, pain of being honest
Let us make it pain for birth for new life
Irresistible urge
That pushes you to seek and ask
Because the given norms are not acceptable

In times of no answer
Your heart burns
Your mind seems to go insane

From time to time
Pretending
That nothing bothers you
Nothing overcomes you

Because there is God
Who is just
Who also suffers
And listens to
Your cries of pain
Your sighs of despair

Let us dare to look up
The sky endless
Even the passing clouds
Are brightly lit
By the mighty sun
And sing the song
Of hope and faith everlasting

Sun Ai Lee Park, Korea

GIVE ME BACK MY WINGS

I've always walked upright
I've seen the sky when it's blue
The flowers in bloom
I've walked past the bent-over woman
but she couldn't see me.

South meets North, so what?
Years ago North first met South
I'm told women could fly back then.

Give me back my wings
That I may once again soar like a bird,
Give me back my wings
That I may rediscover the rooftops
And all that God created me to be.

Where is the bent-over woman?
I look but I cannot see.
... it cannot be?
... that I am the bent over woman?
... could she be me?

God, I wanted to be free.

Fei Taule'ale'ausumai, Aotearoa New Zealand

UNCOVER THE WORD

Layer after layer
the cloth covers the Scripture
like the coming of the Word
to us Filipinos –
    covered by the perceptions of the West,
    covered by the perceptions of men,
    covered by the perceptions of authorities,
    the theologically trained.

I want to read the Word
with you
that my experience of reality
may be in dialogue
with biblical experience
    for enlightenment,
    for strength,
    for affirmation,
    for hope
in the midst of disempowerment,
that together we may form a community of faith.

But first,
uncover the Word!
Remove the cloth that hides it from my understanding,
that keeps me from reading it
with the eyes of my experience.

Uncover the Word
for the reading with new meaning.
Uncover the Word
Uncover the Word.

Cora Tabing-Reyes, Philippines

35

POWERLESS?

My spirit was encased
At birth
within the Female Form.
My role models from childhood
Others encased in the Female Form.

A Female Form
Is powerless,
Economically,
Politically,
Physically,
Religiously,
Domination of the Female Form
Has always been the norm.

But Power exists
When Power is given.
Power controls
When Power is given.
By submission,
By acceptance.
I grant Power
To People
To Systems
To Society
To Structures.

Now my spirit
Re-awakens and revives
As a plant
Crushed within powerful stone
That refuses to be crushed,
But pushes its way,
At first hesitantly,
Then with confidence
To reach out
To the Source of its life – the sun.
I too refuse to abdicate
To grant power
To be crushed.
I reach out exultantly
To the Source of all Life!

Ranjini Rebera, Sri Lanka/Australia

ROLLING WATER

From her four corners
Pachamama
Has sent forth her daughters
Beautiful and strong
Survivors of yesterday
Laden with the heat
And burden of today

Touch her now
The Sister by your side
Feel the pain
Below the joy
Show her the light above
The darkness
Touch her now
The sister in that corner

Listen to her now
The Sister from Africa
Hear the message
Spoken without words
Does it come as Rolling Water
A vibrant sound of life
Or hopelessness
As wind in dry grass?

Listen to her now
The Asian Sister
Weep with her now
The Sister from Latin America

From the four corners
of the *Pachamama*
You the Healers have come

To strengthen the hands
of the Sister from Europe
And bind the wounds
Of your Caribbean Sister

But the moment is fleeting
After today
How can you hold her
The Sister from the Pacific
Reach the North American Sister

Speak to her now
The Sister by your side
Knit a living net
And walk with it
To the Sister
In that corner
Life will spring from the Ashes

For under it is
Pachamama

Walk with her now
The Sister by your side
Walk with her now,
The Sister in that corner.

Nelcia Robinson, St Vincent

WOMEN,
WHY ARE WE STILL
WEEPING?

WOMEN, WHY ARE WE STILL WEEPING?

And Jesus said follow me
> and we walked together the road
> where the Canaanite women struggled
> trying to be heard, understood, taken seriously

>> and he told me about her way
>> let them not push you down
>> ask and argue
>> keep shouting
>> just don't give up!

And Jesus said follow me
> and he took me to the home of the two sisters
> called Martha and Mary
> and asked me to learn from their argument

>> let not any given role
>> shrink your talents
>> let not any cultural rule
>> squeeze you
>> just respond to your call
>> in all its fullness!

And Jesus said follow me
> and he showed me the room
> where he was treated as the One
> he is being anointed by a woman
> and he told me
> that even his closest friends
> became irritated by her behaviour
> advised her to be more rational

>> but he asked me to remember her
>> as my own ancestor
>> trust in your instincts
>> see what you already sense
>> dare to feel
>> just act in your faith

And Jesus said follow me
and he sat with me at the well
told me about a Samaritan woman
who was straightforward
engaged in a theological dialogue with him
spoke up in her city
what she had understood
and he told me that many in that city
believed in him because of the
testimony of this woman

and he asked me to respect this woman
ask your questions
they all are worthy of answers
let not anything in your past
become a prison to you
don't be afraid to share
what you have discovered
just see your change, take it
open up for a new task!

And Jesus said follow me
and he stayed with me
in the garden of the Easter morning
empty tomb,
the stone, rolled away
absence and presence all mixed
and he looked at me,
repeated his first sentence as a risen Christ
"Women, why are you weeping?"
Women, why are we still weeping?

Irja Askola, Finland

WHAT DOES IT MEAN?

What does it mean
When the sun rises,
the cold rain leaves
and the dove of peace comes,

Is that a sign of – *freedom*?

What does it mean
When the field...
in the sky a rainbow forms,
"Don't let them kill your father",

Is that a sign of – *love*?

What does it mean
When the war is no more,
flowers burst into bloom,
and bullets no longer fall like rain,

Is that a sign of – *happiness*?

What does it mean
When the golden lilies
from blood will blossom,

Is that a sign of – *freedom, love and happiness*?

Bosnia is a part of me
That is hidden deep in my soul.
Bosnia is some happy child
that, like the sea, swims across the land.
Bosnia is these mountains
Bosnia is the clean rivers and forests,
Bosnia is the greatest, most wonderful love
    which, like a secret, never ceases to grow.
Bosnia is my heart
Bosnia is my soul.
Bosnia is a golden grain of sand
    which, from my hand, shall never fall.

Lajla Talovic, Bosnia

WOMEN WHO BEAR THE PAIN
OVER LIFE THAT IS WASTED IN WAR

Life is conceived in a womb
Protected in a seeming crystal bowl
Blood, love and hope are mingled together
to let this life behold the dawn.

But a sudden flash of light
dropped out of arrogance and might
transforms this valuable being
into ashes of smoke, if not into
the crippled, and wounded
invalids throughout their lives.

How the women groan!
How the mothers die a thousand deaths!
When life that is nurtured
from womb to the dawn of light
is shattered in a wasteland.

Elizabeth Padillo-Olesen, Netherlands

Remembering the Struggle and Grief of Indigenous Women's Lives

How are we to be women clothed with the sun?
Can we be women clothed with the Australian sun,
concerned for our own growth and development,
while the original women of the Australian sun
live in the desert of racism,
their human rights
systematically abused and denied by our nation
which claims it is a champion of human rights?

How are we to be women clothed with the sun
in a nation giving birth to a republic
and a multi-cultural society,
while the original women of the Australian sun
see their male children
taken not to God upon his throne,
not to safety and honour,
but to juvenile detention centres
and to cells where their souls are destroyed
and they seek peace in suicide,
if they are not murdered first?
For whatever you do to the least of these
you do to me, Christ said.
And so our nation murders the child
time and time again,
or leaves the child to die from neglect.

How are we to be women clothed in the sun,
while the colours yellow, red and black
have ambiguous meanings for us?

Yellow is for celebration.
But can we celebrate
as long as Aboriginal communities
know the yellow of jaundice
because of disease
which damages communities
who have not been provided with
adequate water and sewerage
or whose new houses
have toilets connected to kitchen sinks?

Red is for joy and pain.
But can we use red for joy
as long as we do not make amends
for the red blood
of Aboriginal men and women
that flowed in massacres which drove the people from the land
and enforced our cultural and economic claims?

Black is for strength, depth and power.
But can we use black
while we collaborate with a culture
which assumes black represents evil
and white good?
Can we use black,
while strength, depth and power

are used by white culture to enforce its ways
on Indigenous women of the sun,
their children
and their men?

The original women of the Australian sun,
women whose flag is yellow, red and black,
have eagles' wings
or else they would not survive
our racist, materialist, hypocritical
"culture"
which is
the huge red dragon with seven heads
and ten horns.

Australian women and men
now have three human rights reports
from Michael Dodson,
one black, one yellow, one red.
They are disturbing reports
of our nation and our culture,
more about the black and yellow of bruises
and the blood red of lives cut short
than about celebration, joy, strength or depth.
What will we non-Indigenous women
do with these reports?
Will we continue as part of the beast,
or will we join the women of the sun
in the desert,
where Aboriginal wisdom
has been able to live
through millennia
in harmony with the life-giving earth?

Will we reject the beast
and find in the colours of these reports
the invitation
to live for our sisters and ourselves?
What does our God require of us?
Do justice, love mercy,
walk humbly with God.
Save the child.
Believe that the beast
can be vanquished
and the child live:
a new nation of justice.

The problem is we cannot simply turn from the beast
to the desert.
The beast of institutionalized
Australian racism
must be destroyed.
That takes more than stories,
more than creative thinking,
more than evocative colours.

Ann Wansborough, Australia

O, Women of Asia

Holding a lantern in her hand

awaken this long night
in silence strewn with
thousands of hopes and wishes
yet unspoken, yet unfolded
Asian women
await the dawning of another day

She knows the pains of labour
She stands proud and meek
in the noble traditions
of culture and great civilization
humane and full of wisdom
thirsting for eternal truth and mercy

These children of hers
for whom she gave
all of herself
not asking reward
nor expecting recognition
she devotes all of herself
to give life
to provide
to nurture
to make men and women
and to pass her own task
of many a burden
as she returns quietly
to the eternal cycle
of death and rebirth
as if she had never been there
as if she had taken no part
in the history and civilization
of great harmony and peace
as she fades away
like a shadow
like a vapour

O, women of Asia
in her silence patiently waits
the dawning of another day
a lantern in her hand
vigilant in this pitch-dark night
of muscular dominations
which kill tender lives
in pain she gave birth
and all that she holds dearest

O, women of Asia
It's time to say "No!"
To all destructive forces of domination
and "Yes!" to the freedom journey

The Lord of history has opened a new chapter
Let us live through the night
to live wholly
in the morning to come
in the days ahead.

Sun Ai Lee Park, Korea

WOMEN OF ZAMBIA

We have read an account in the scriptures of a woman who for eighteen years was crippled with infirmity. She was bent over for eighteen years. I want us to see the state of this woman. She could not achieve that which her intellect and her mind desired. She couldn't get to the heights that every other woman desired to get to. She was crippled. All she could see day after day was the floor. She couldn't stand up straight at all. Then one day, this woman walked into the Temple and Jesus was there. She could have pretended she didn't hear him, that Jesus was talking to somebody else. Fear would have gripped her. How do I get up, move through all these indignant men? And many of us, like her, are gripped with fear.

Women of Zambia, hear me. Be free from that fear. Let your capabilities be seen. Let us stand and be a blessing to our nation. I believe it with all my heart that if there is an asset that any nation or any people has it is its women. We are the centre – hallelujah! We are to make, to build. Be freed!

God wants us to soar. But we can only soar in the heights if our spirit and mind are released and freed from bondage. That's when God will hear us. Like this woman who recognized that *the one who has called me is greater than the rulers of the synagogue*. We have got to realize that God is greater than anything else. That is why I cry out to the church to stand together with the women.

I cry out to the church to get hold of God!

Nawa Phiri, Zambia

A DECADE LAMENT

How Long O God How Long?
How long must women
bear suffering on earth?
Hagar, Jephthah's daughter, Rizpah, Susanna, Tamar, Mary.
Their stories, God, repeated in every generation,
make a mockery of claims of justice and equality.
How long O God must we wait?

How Long O God How Long
must we endure
the spirit of those who sacrifice
women's life and liberation to war, culture, order,
stilted hierarchy and ecclesial traditions?

How long must we wait for the days when
unjust judges, fed up with the importunity
of widows, single mothers
and immigrant women,
give in and let justice prevail?

How long must we wait O God
for the fullness of community
where young girls no longer crouch
in bedroom corners in fear of a father's touch,
where battered women no longer cringe
with the thought of a husband's return,
where women in love with women
no longer live with shame and fear of ridicule,
where a man's touch of women
is no longer neglectful of indifference, and dignity?

How Long O God How Long?
How long will our statistics go on
screaming messages of abuse, prejudice, harassment?
A Decade, two decades, a century?
What time extension do we give God, and will you allow
in Your world to
the fact that
in this country 55 percent of single elderly women are poor,
to the fact that 81 percent of rapes or attempted rapes
are perpetrated by men known to women,
to the fact that 96 percent of those who sexually abuse children are
men,
to the fact that women are paid less than 75 cents for every dollar
paid to men for full employment, and so on...?

Mother/Father God, hear us
as we cry out in protest and anguish.
With Gethsemane – like spirit and feelings of God-forsakenness
we too beg, demand, insist that the cup be removed,
that it be taken away,
for we know now,
this side of the resurrection faith,
that it is not your will for women to endure oppression,
that you have no heaven where
women live outside the image of your created goodness,
and so it shall not be so on earth.

We now know, O God, that with your Spirit we have an advocate.
We have in the Spirit of Jesus a Friend.
But where, O God, do we find on earth that friendship,
friendship that is willing to
travel through forbidden territory,
stop at traditional wells and talk
to untraditional women, that refuses to condemn,
or throw stones with male accusers,
that can be open to women's gifts of oil,
of good news running from empty tombs,
that can affirm the healing wholeness of women's faith?
Where, O God, where
do we find that friendship which
gives place to your feminine side,
your spirit of conceiving and giving birth,
your maternal compassion for the weak, and sick, and oppressed?

Where, O God, where
are those on earth willing to seek rebirth
through the "amniotic waters of baptism"
and be gathered under
the mothering-hen wings of your care and love.

We await, O God, the day of your coming
when you will pour out your Spirit on all flesh,
when your daughters shall prophesy,
old men dream dreams, and young men see visions,
when your will on earth is done as in heaven.
We await the day, O God,
when your grace and peace abound,
when all together will walk on holy ground.

But for God's sake,
don't make it too long!!

Hallett Llewellyn, Canada

HOW CAN WE SING A NEW SONG?

How
can we sing a new song from
the valley of shards?
We are broken vessels
in a fissured land, indeed
we can hear
the parchment earth crack open
beneath our feet even
as we speak.

What
can we do *except*
sing songs of protest, lamentation, hope
from split and bleeding lips
in the valley of splintered dreams?
What, except believe
that earth, like a fragile egg
cracks open to expose
new quiverings of life?

Kate Compston, England

THE JUSTICE
OF WOMEN'S LIBERATION

THE JUSTICE OF WOMEN'S LIBERATION

The justice of women's liberation, I establish hereby. If you deny liberation to women, there is no more life in this world. In your cunningness to control your wife, can you relegate the entire humanity of women as slaves?

Bharathi, India

VERONICA

According to the ancient traditions of the church, when our Lord was carrying his cross his face could not be recognized because of the blood and sweat mixed with dust and dirt on it. Then a woman by the name of Veronica went forward, and with her handkerchief cleansed the face and made it possible once more for the real countenance to be seen.

Men and women are made in God's image. God's face in them is so often unrecognized because of all kinds of dirt on them. But she of whom I speak cleansed many a face in Iran; one of them being my own. That is why I thank God for her and people like her..., and my prayer is that their like may be increased.

Bishop Hassan Dehqani-Tafti, Iran

RENCONTRE

Femme, nous avons deviné tes larmes,
blessure de l'âme,
larmes
en ta dignité cachées:
La douleur a durci ton visage
sans âge.
Ta voix dure et ferme
nous a conté la vie broyée, si tôt.
Femme, mère, Epouse,
victime de la cruauté du système
qui veut que la pauvreté
nourrisse la richesse des nantis,
femme, c'est nous qui avons pleuré.
Toi tu n'avais qu'un cri
tu voulais du travail
et nos bras étaient lourds d'impuissance.
Mère d'enfants marqués jusqu'en leur corps
par la violence,
tu veux te battre
pour les protéger.
D'âge, on ne pouvait t'en donner.
Devant ta dignité
on s'est incliné:

Nous ne pouvions que prier et t'embrasser

dans une même tendresse;

Mais au combat pour la justice, tu nous as renvoyés.

Femme,

tu nous as remplis de ta révolte.

Avec tes sœurs tu nous as rappelé

qu'il n'est de dignité sans justice

qu'il n'est de foi vivante

sans amour ni tendresse.

André Jacques, France

WOMEN AND MEN ARE PARTNERS

Human community is possible only with women and men. The kingdom is possible for men only with women. Along with committed men, who do not aspire to dominate, they are the ones who help sustain human values to permeate the society. Enduring values in life – sharing, peace, harmony – are the things they strive for. They have distinct contributions to make. That is, they are the ones who can humanize us and bring some sense and order into this chaotic world. Women seek drastic changes in the structures of society and they have a vision for a new earth and a new heaven. In this they seek dialogue with concerned men. They seek to communicate in order to be able to be understood aright. They wish to be recognized as persons in their own right. They struggle in order to be human, and it is in this struggle that men should join hands with them and struggle together. For men's liberation is dependent on women's liberation. As long as men dominate and oppress women, they themselves are not free and liberated beings.

Women in different contexts today struggle for humanity, dignity, identity, equality and survival; and they are concerned about justice, peace and love. They yearn to celebrate the God of creation and life. In other words, they are seeking a dialogue with men – their fathers, lovers or husbands and sons who, in actual life-situations, are their oppressors. Their oppressors are there also in the church, in the work-place and in the society at large.

Jesus, the God incarnate, though living in a male-dominated patriarchal society, could still accept women as they were. He helped them, enabled them, empowered them and employed them powerfully in his ministry. He even challenged his patriarchal society. Anyone who wishes to establish a new earth and a new heaven must certainly emulate Jesus' paradigm.

Women and men are partners with God. Man has to accept this basic theological affirmation or remain condemned.

Franklyn J. Balasundaram, India

THREE POEMS

OUR CHILDREN

We have two children: a stone girl
and a space-age boy...

Our electric boy is quick, bright
sharp as lightning and eloquent.
His appetite for constant amusement
and titillation is insatiable.

Each Christmas his requests are legion:
a laser gun, digital watch, remote control car
and kit for space invasion.
But don't give me food as presents,
he admonishes, they soon disappear.
You can't play with food, he reckons.

No, you cannot play with food,
our little stone girl will agree

as gargoyle-like she crouches
in unsmiling wide-eyed silence

Empty bowl in tiny brittle hands
whittled to bone by malnutrition.

She has no dreams of toys
and asks for nothing;
but the hunger
(not metaphorical) in her eye
says all there is to say:
the only gift I and my seventeen million
other brothers and sisters need each year

is urgent loving care and a full belly
or we may, all of us, soon disappear...

LITTLE FLOWER

Your arrival was unplanned
unscheduled, you burst
into the afternoon of
our already mapped-out lives

and Life was chaos
for a short while...
We had to shift beds
rearrange the furniture
to accommodate you
tiny stranger from nowhere

But it was worthwhile
already you illuminate
our humdrum mornings
with your gurgling smile
bubbly companion to your brother
little flower that blossomed in late October.

YOUR EYES

Since you came
your eyes
have awakened mine
taught them to see

Never knew
such magic
in a simple blade
of grass
such laughter
in the crackle of a
newspaper
such horror
in a single departure

With you
everything's wonder
adventure
a door knob, a gear
the contents of a bin
a red umbrella
reflections in a mirror
bubbles dancing on water

I shall never again
be bored, be lonely
learning as you do
to converse not only
with dog, flower, tree
but also with calendar
powderpuff & safety-pin
an old bit of string
a bunch of jangling keys

You have taught me
joy, intensity
curiosity
terror, adventure
laughter
You have shattered
complacency
Since you came
my life
has been touched
by yours
my eyes awakened
by yours
before you came
they were only
open
couldn't really see

Cecil Rajendra, Malaysia

I AM A WOMAN

Don't call me a man – I am a woman

When I disagree with you
You say I am big-headed

When I refuse your advances
You say I am arrogant

When I just keep quiet
You say I am proud

Don't call me a man – I am a woman

When I give my suggestions
You say education has spoiled me

When I stand to speak
You say I lack respect

When I demand my rights
You say the women's guild has spoiled me

Don't call me a man – I am a woman

When I challenge a man's ideas
You say I'm masculine

When I vie for leadership
you say I'm a man

When I address a *barraza*
You say I should put on men's trousers

Don't call me a man – I am a woman

I am a woman
with all my ways
I am a woman
So!

Don't call me a man

Bantu Mwaura, Kenya

HOUSE MAID

She worked in her neighbour's house
Long hair crossing her waist.
In modest dress with inert movement
Never looked pale in her sweet glance

    The children in the house
    Much younger than she
    Call her in a loud voice
    As if they are much older

The master and his wife
At the top of their voice
Call her now and then
Give orders as they wish

    She takes meals separately
    Lonely when others have finished
    Her bed is on the floor
    In the kitchen or in the corridor

Keeping aside all dirt and shoes
She puts her rag
And fixes the net with so many patches
And a flat pillow

She wakes up while others are still asleep
Sweeps the rooms
Cleans the courtyard
Washes utensils and the kids as well

    The work list is long
    When others are out
    On the weekend
    She remains busy washing clothes
    A few moments often she has
    Sweet moments of her own
    She sinks into deep thought
    A village flashes in her eyes

A village appears and a home
The widow mother, a house maid too
And starving brothers and sisters
Looking for the favour of God.

Abdus Sabur, Bangladesh

WAKING UP FROM SLUMBER

We have to face the reality that women are discriminated against within the church and within the African tradition. Within both traditions we argue at a theoretical level that men and women are equal, but many things at a practical level continue to undermine and contradict that affirmation. Do the structures of our church governance reflect the reality that the overwhelming majority of our church membership is women? How are women consulted when the most burning issues of the doctrine and governance of the church are being debated and legislated on? How much of the gospel proclamation is done in our churches by women – not only by women to other women, but also by women to both men and women, and even by women to men? I know a number of men who are struggling with the exclusivity in our language, especially in our reading of the liturgy, with its one-sidedly male image of God – the "Almighty Father, King, Lord and Master of mankind" sort of language. But how many of us are working seriously at finding alternatives and revising the liturgy itself to be more gender-sensitive?

The theology of liberation started to make a serious contribution to our understanding of the Christian faith when the oppressed themselves began to articulate their understanding of God on the basis of their own personal experience of being oppressed. A similar contribution can come when the church creates a space for more women theologians to articulate their understanding of faith from the perspective of women. Seminaries, theological colleges and universities must make room in theology faculties for women to practise, to teach and to be involved in training those who are going to be ministers in the church.

When liberation theology began to develop in South Africa, I recall how heretical some of what was being said sounded to our white brothers and sisters in the church – that God is black or that God has a bias in favour of black people as victims of discrimination. But the liberation of theology itself was born out of such apparently heretical statements. I believe space must be created – especially perhaps by those of us who were the heretics of yesterday – for similar "heresies" in the area of gender issues to be articulated in our pulpits, in our conference halls, in our lecture theatres. Until such statements are made to shock and dismay, we are not likely to wake up from our slumber.

Bongani Blessing Finca, South Africa

THE GOSPEL
ACCORDING TO YOU

THE GOSPEL ACCORDING TO YOU

There is a wonderful old story
Written in a time long gone.
It is the gospel according to
Matthew, Mark, Luke and John.

The gospels were given to show us
The power of God's love divine.
May that story be told again
In the writing of your life and mine.

People read and admire the gospel,
With its love so inspiring and true,
But what do they say and think of
The gospel according to you?

We are writing a gospel,
A chapter every day,
By deeds that we do,
By words that we say.

We are writing each day a gospel.
Take care that the writing is true,
For the only gospel some will read
Is the gospel according to you.

Author Unknown

GOD IS WEAVING

God is crying.
The tapestry
that she wove with such joy
is mutilated, torn,
made into pieces
its beauty torn apart with violence.

God is crying.
But see!
She is gathering the pieces
to weave something new.

She collects
the pieces from hard work

> the aim to defend the initiative for peace
> the protests against injustice
> everything that seems small and weak
> words and deeds given
> as sacrifice in hope, in belief, in love

And see!
She is weaving them together
with the golden threads of joy to a new tapestry
a creation richer, more beautiful than the old!

God is weaving
patient, persistent

> with a smile
> that is shimmering like a rainbow
> over her face, striped with tears
> And she invites us not only to continue
> to give her our works
> and our suffering pieces.

> But even more –
> to sit beside her
> at the loom of Jubilee
> and weave together with her
> the Tapestry of A New Creation

Yvonne Dahlin, Sweden

CHRIST COMES TO US WOMEN TODAY!

This we believe in, that Jesus accompanies us women in our everyday experiences of life and in our struggles to find justice and a violence-free world. It is a faith that knows no boundaries, a faith that sustains us in our struggles for life. Jesus is that theology of life – God with us.

Christ came to us women today,
He celebrated with us our small victories.
A poem we wrote together, rather than spend endless times weeping.
A song of liberation we sang together, as we walked another mile.
A theology of resurrection we wrote together, as we deconstructed all that is unjust.
A dance of freedom we danced, dancing away all that creates disharmony and causes us rage.
Christ came to us women today,
He promised to walk that journey with us...

Christ came to her, my sister, today,
He wept with her as she wept tears of pain.
A poem of love he wrote to her to remind her that God cares.
A song of liberation he sang for her, challenging her to reclaim her power.
A dance of freedom he danced with her, giving her the strength to stand up and dance.
Christ came to us women today,
He promised to walk that journey with us...

Christ came to the church today,
He wept for her seeing her lack of courage and strength,
A poem of love he wrote for her, to remind her of his passion and compassion.
A song of liberation he sang to awaken her to his message of salvation for all.
A theology of resurrection he wrote when he called us to live in right relationships.
A dance of freedom he danced with us, challenging us to stand up and dance for him.
Christ came to the church today,
He promised to walk that journey with us.

Aruna Gnanadason, India

THE STORY OF JOANNA
(Luke 8:3; 24:10)

In the Greek scriptures, women gave strong, consistent leadership to the emerging Christian community. However, their contributions were not given the same importance as those of the male disciples. This history needs to be recovered because it is women's history today – it is our story.

Women associated themselves with Jesus from the start. Jesus restored many women to health, community and wholeness. He enabled them to give equal leadership with men in the community. To "be cured of evil spirits and infirmities" did not necessarily mean that the women were sick or had been healed from physical diseases, or that they followed Jesus simply out of gratitude. Lee Oo Chung, a South Korean theologian, points out that the Greek word *therapeuo*, which means to heal a disease, is *not* the word used in Luke 8:2. Rather, the Greek word *apolouo* is used, which means "to be set free" – in these instances from the types of bondage that inhibit women's full maturity.

Some of these women supported Jesus with "their resources". At the cross, when the male disciples fled, the women remained to mourn. They were the first to experience the resurrection and to spread the good news, although they were not believed. As the early Christian community grew, women preached alongside men, went on missionary journeys, directed communities, taught the children and hosted house churches. Yet much of this early history has not been highlighted in the Greek scriptures. As a result, it appears as though it was only men who gave major leadership. In her work with the gospels and the letters of Paul, Elisabeth Schüssler Fiorenza finds evidence for an early Jesus movement that was thoroughly egalitarian and included powerful women.

Joanna was one of these women. An obscure figure, the wife of Herod's steward Chuza, she appears two or three times in the records. She supports Jesus "with her resources", mourns him on the cross and is present with the other women at the empty tomb. She has a political background, being associated by marriage with Herod's corrupt and adulterous court.

We do not know if Joanna "left all" and followed Jesus as did the male disciples. If she did so, she would have caused a scandal in patriarchal society. The male disciples, on the other hand, were commended for their swift response to Jesus' call. We do not know that she remained at the cross when the men had fled. She went to anoint the body of Jesus, while the male disciples hid in despair.

Her story is important because it illustrates one of the many women whose life was transformed from death to life through Jesus. In that sense her story is our story. It is important for children to know the stories of women like Joanna, as well as the stories of Peter, James and John and the male disciples.

Lois Wilson, Canada

A TRIBUTE TO RIZPAH:
A SPIRITUALITY OF RESISTANCE AND
TRANSFORMATION

Any spirituality that does not lead to engagement in the making of peace, the crafting of non-violent responses to contemporary events and relationships, is not worthy of being called a spirituality (Megan McKenna, *Not Counting Women and Children*, Maryknoll NY, Orbis Books, 1994, p.204).

My name is Rizpah, daughter of Aiah,
Secret lover of King Saul, the first king
    of the people of Israel
Never mind that the biographer of King Saul
    and David calls me a concubine
As usual, because I am a woman, he never
consulted me when he wrote about me
Listen to my story

King Saul and I were great lovers
Together we had two sons,
    Armoni and Mephibosheth
During those intimate moments,
my lover poured his heart out to me
He hated war
He hated bloodshed
Guilt feelings overtook his joy
    and love for life
He would weep all night long after the battle

He told me how badly he felt after
    all that bloodshed.
Yet, he had to secure territories
    for his people
The day he met his death,
    he had expressed his fear
    that I would not see him again
We held each other and cried endlessly

During those intimate moments
He spoke endlessly about Samuel,
    the prophet who anointed him
David he despised and wished
    they never met
He spoke tenderly
about Samuel's mother, Hannah
A loving and dedicated mother
Oh how I wished I had met her

From Hannah's story,
I learned about a merciful God
A God who listened to women
Hannah's story taught me
how to weep for the unborn
For the dying and the dead
The day my lover died
no one could console me
Silently, I bore the pain
        of losing my lover

I was afraid,
they would kill my sons too
Dumb and deaf I became
In shame, I hid my face
My lover's body was put up for display
Silently, I wept and bore the shame
Days, months, years
I cried to the God of Hannah
God of Hannah and Samuel, have mercy
God was very angry
Bloodshed, revenge, bloodshed

My sons too fell to the cruel hands
        of the enemies
Enough is enough
On a sackcloth, I kept vigil
Birds, animals, flies and dust,
I kept away
Away with evil, away with death,
        away with bloodshed
No more silence, no more war
Shout, cry out, actions speak louder than words
Away with evil, away with bloodshed,
        away with death

You know what, many years later
Another woman watched her son die
She too resisted evil, death and bloodshed
Sisters, away with evil, death and bloodshed
Enough is enough
Away with war, revenge, death, bloodshed
Let the mighty kings and dictators shake
Let them shake in their graves
Shout, let the earth quake
Let there be life, let there be peace

Sisters, at the cross, the struggle continues!
In Africa, my sisters keep vigil
2000 years later, they will sit at the cross
Away with genocide, away with revenge,
      away with rape
Our sons are murdered, our daughters are raped
Mothers of Africa still keep vigil at the cross

At the cross they cry out for mercy
God of Hannah, Rizpah, Mary
Save our land from self-destruction
Enough is enough
Away with the machete, land mines, guns
Away with the knife,
Let our girls enjoy their childhood
      and their womanhood
Give peace and life a chance
Mothers and daughters of Africa
Hannah, Rizpah, Mary
      accompany you in your struggle
You are not alone
The vigil continues, at the cross!

Nyambura Njoroge, Kenya

THE LIFE OF ST NINA

Born in Cappadocia in the late third century, St Nina was the only daughter of the Roman general Zabulon and his wife Susanna. When Nina was 12, her family travelled to Jerusalem where, with the patriarch's blessing, her father became a monk, her mother became a church worker, and Nina became the foster child of Nianfora, a pious elderly woman. Under the tutelage of her foster mother, Nina quickly learned the rules of faith and piety.

At 14, Nina questioned her mentor about the location of Christ's robe. Nina felt that such an important relic could not have been lost. Nianfora told her that it was in Iberia (now Georgia), a land not yet completely illumined. When the apostles had drawn lots to determine who was to preach where, the Theotokos came to Nina and urged her to preach the gospel in Georgia. The Mother of God assured Nina that she would protect her and, as a pledge, left a cross of grape vines.

The patriarch, her uncle, was delighted with the news of her vision and eagerly gave her his blessing:

Lord God, our Saviour! As I let this young girl depart to preach thy divinity, I commit her into thy hands. Condescend, O Christ God, to be her Companion and Teacher everywhere, so that she proclaims thy Good Tidings, and give her words with such force and wisdom that no one will be able to oppose or refute them. And thou, most Holy Virgin Mother of God, Helper and Intercessor for all Christians, clothe with thy strength against all enemies, visible and invisible, this girl whom thou thyself hast chosen to preach the gospel of thy Son and our God among the pagan nations. Be always for her a shield and an invisible protection, and do not deprive her of thy favour until she has fulfilled thy holy will.

Nina joined the party of Princess Ripsimia, which was travelling to Georgia to escape the persecution of Diocletian. All but Nina, who was sheltered in a crevice, were martyred in Armenia after Ripsimia declined to marry the king, Tiridat.

Living as a pilgrim, by the grace of God and on the bounty of strangers, Nina once became weary. She wondered briefly where she was going, what she was doing. Exhausted, she fell asleep and had a vision of a majestic man who handed her a scroll in Greek, which she read upon waking:

Verily, I say unto you, "Wheresoever this gospel shall be preached in the whole world, there shall also this, which this woman has done, be told as a memorial to her (Matthew 26:13). *There is neither Jew nor Greek, there is neither bond nor free, there is neither male nor female; for you are all one in Christ Jesus*" (Galatians 3:28).

Strengthened and reassured, Nina continued until she arrived in Georgia, where she witnessed the worship of the local gods. Praying that the idols might be destroyed, she also witnessed a downpour that washed the idols into the river.

Nina settled in Mtskheta, the capital, where she lived in a hut near the royal gardener and his wife Anastasia. There Nina gained a reputation for holiness both because of her daily piety and her miraculous healings. She cured Queen Nana of a disease no doctor had been able to relieve. King Mirian was converted when he was saved from a rainstorm similar to the one that had destroyed his idols.

After preaching to and converting many Jews and pagans, Nina learned the story of Christ's robe: a local Jew, Elioz, had obtained the robe from the soldier to whose lot it had fallen and had carried it home to Georgia. His sister Sidonia had clasped the robe to her breast and had died. No one could take the robe from her, and it had been buried with her. A cedar, now part of the royal garden, was said to have grown from her grave. Nina had doubts about the identification of the particular tree, but she knew from her visions that the ground was holy.

Nina died in the early fourth century, after she had seen Christianity spread through Georgia and had, through her preaching, converted a neighbouring queen, Sophia of Kakhetian, and her kingdom. Nina was buried near the place where she had died in Bodbi. The church built by her grave was dedicated to St George and became the Bodbi metropolitanate. Her cross was sent to the cathedral in Mtskheta. During wars between the Byzantine and Persian empires, the cross was taken to Armenia and eventually to Moscow. Tsar Alexander I returned it to Georgia at the beginning of the nineteenth century.

Karen Keck, USA

St Brigit

St Brigit was the abbess of a large double monastery in Kildare, Ireland. She lived in the fifth and early sixth centuries.

St Brigit was not known to be passive. She has been extolled by her biographers as a person who was sometimes unpredictable by human standards and always full of life. She was well known as an advocate of the lowly. In many of the miraculous stories about her, St Brigit is depicted as being a "personification of compassion". From her youth, there are numerous accounts describing her unusual generosity and concern for the poor. She was also deeply revered as a wise "soul friend" to many. She was even known to befriend wild animals.

Brigit was particularly renowned for her psychological wholeness, her clarity of mind and a radical grounding in God. This foundation allowed her to rise above the apparent constrictions of the day. It is her inner spiritual integrity for which she is most remembered. As a Spirit-bearer, St Brigit was a person of prayer and a "friend of God" or *philotheos*. This is evidenced by a recurrent theme in the hagiographical stories about her.

On the day that Brigit was to be received into monastic life, something remarkable occurred. It was perhaps because of her great humility, born out of her deep communion with God, that Brigit quietly placed herself at the end of the line of the sisters being received. The bishop, who was to confer the monastic tonsure, was also revered as a holy man. On seeing Brigit, he witnessed that "a fiery pillar rose from her head to the roof of the church".

We in the Eastern Christian tradition would recognize these words as referring to someone who was in a state of glorification, or *theosis*. Being participants in what we Orthodox call "the uncreated glory of God in Christ" they become "the only authorities within the Orthodox Church". In other words, those human persons who have the final authority in the church are those who have been glorified, the saints. This reality is at the heart of Orthodox theology.

Theology, while academically accountable, is essentially pastoral or therapeutic in nature. The purpose of good theology concerns far more than an accurate articulation of belief, vital as this is. At the same time, faithful articulation of theology is quite literally vital. This is because authentic doctrinal formulations "serve as guides to the cure of the centre of the human personality and as warning signs to stay away from quack doctors who promise much and have nothing to give in preparation for the experience of God's glory in Christ...".

With this in mind, we can appreciate how Brigit's godly bishop, through divine inspiration, recognized that she had already become a "temple of the Holy Spirit" (1 Corinthians 6:19). He bade her to come forward from her last place in line in order to be admitted into monastic life first. Then, in response to the Holy Spirit, he received her, not with the invocation for the tonsuring of a nun or monk, but with the ordination prayer of a bishop.

The bishop's assistant was shocked and enraged by this. He stressed that "a bishop's rank should not be conferred on a woman". To this, the discerning bishop replied, "But I do not have any power in this matter. That dignity has been given by God to Brigit." And from that time on "episcopal honour" was given to her successors in the monastery.

While it is unusual, we Orthodox today would not be too surprised that the ancient church recognized Brigit as a living saint in this way. The unique manner in which she was received into monastic life signifies the public recognition that Brigit was among the glorified. She expressed the fullness of prophetic authority in the church as she "knew God".

The actions of St Brigit's holy bishop also serve as a powerful example to us. Through spiritual discernment, he felt compelled to respond to the will of God. Furthermore, his part in the story demonstrates that we must strive to avoid distractions when seeking "the one thing necessary" (Luke 10:42). The manner by which this man of God peacefully supported his actions in the face of angry opposition is an invitation for many of us to do likewise.

The humble confession of Brigit's discerning bishop, "I do not have any power in this matter", furthermore indicates that the unceasing prayer which beats in his heart may have been, "Not my will, but your will, be done" (Matthew 26:39). Today, this prayer also bids us to respond faithfully to the presence of God in our own lives and in relationship with others. Furthermore, as believers, it is our responsibility – or, perhaps more precisely, our privilege – faithfully to search, test, recognize and affirm "that dignity which has been given by God" to all his holy servants, both male and female.

Kyriaki Karidoyanes FitzGerald, USA

ICON PAINTING AS DEVOTION AND DISCIPLINE

In sight of the Green Mountains of Vermont and enclosed within the liturgical richness of matins and vespers at New Skete Monastery, I have spent a number of weeks attempting to capture the likeness of Theotokos with the use of egg, water, pigment and wood... I have come to a profound appreciation for the devotion and discipline required to portray a holy face.

The painting, or writing, of icons is a spiritual exercise, requiring first of all love of God. We can paint authentically only what we truly love. The icon painter must have a profound devotion to our Lord, his Mother and the saints, and must be engaged in a life of personal and corporate prayer. This is essential in order to attempt to portray the likeness.

Further, love of neighbour is necessary to motivate the iconographer to keep the likeness clean and free of ego, so that the painter is out of the way, does not intrude and allows the image to confront the viewer as directly as possible.

Icon painting is not only a devotion but also a discipline. The devotion and commitment to God are essential for motivation and desire; the discipline is essential to hone one's talents and focus one's ability to bring about the appropriate image.

The iconographer must accept the canonical rules of iconographic painting, submitting herself to them. Having come from some experience with water-colours, in which the unpredictable flow of the water creates a certain quixotic beauty, I learned that quite a different approach is required with icons. Icon painting involves the building up of "lights" in which brush strokes are not seen on the areas of the face. In water-colour, the evidence of the brush, in many instances, is highly desirable.

However, the allegiance to structure and rules must be balanced by a surrender to the Holy Spirit, who guides the artist. Icons should never be slavish copies but should express a balance which integrates a particular manifestation of the Spirit and the classic rules of icon painting.

There were many exciting and challenging moments in the limited icon painting experience that I had: learning the technique of lights, in which one layers on wash after wash of ochre to build up the planes of the face, with the final lights bringing the face fully into form; the critical task of defining the eyes, which at a certain point begin looking back at you; the careful modelling of the mouth to keep the expression serene, gentle, yet firm and strong; the challenge of portraying the Babe as vulnerable, yet not infantile.

There is also much symbolism in the painting process. Again, the layering and building up of the lights reminds one of our gradual "enlightenment" as we attempt to grow towards God. The richness of the final portrait, which holds such depth, points to the mystery of the human person who is ultimately unfathomable except to God. This was a particularly vivid realization as I attempted to portray the face of the Mother of God who, in response to Gabriel's message, surrendered into the infinite freedom to become all she was called to become and who is the perfect paradigm of the response to God as he calls us into his life.

At the completion of the icon of the Theotokos, it was apparent that the gold leaf of the background and halo, as well as the final oil finish, which deepened and enriched the colours, seemed to move the icon into another dimension. At some point in this process, I surrendered "ownership" and began to understand true synergeia. Pat Reid's wonderful pedagogy, my struggling efforts and the Holy Spirit came together to make the wood, egg, water, oil and pigment a holy work, providing a glimpse of the Transcendent on which the window opens slightly to reveal a hint of the awesome beauty of Truth.

Nancy Holloway, USA

SURPRISED BY JOY

As an artist, what I found initially irresistible about Christianity was this all-consuming fire, a love as strong as death... I worried that becoming Christian would mean the end of creativity, that I would lose the pagan instincts that fire the imagination and the primitive urges to heights of creative power in art, poetry and music... But in relenting to the stark gospel of the Cross, I was surprised by the joyful relief of divine humour and knew the absolute futility of the devil's lies. My art didn't perish; I only stopped being a "mere" artist. To be converted to faith is to step into a realm of paradoxes and take on an even more relentless engagement with life, too intense even for art...

I love to think of clay as the most apt poetic metaphor for artistic creation. It is a very sensuous medium – soft, obedient and pleasurable to the touch. The artist is in most immediate contact with it, working directly with hands and body.

I derive almost childlike delight working in this medium, remembering the time in childhood when playing with dirt and mud was such a grievous misdeed. Clay is a natural plaything and touching it revives old instincts. The thing is to let them out as fast as I can, spontaneously and joyously.

I liken the potter to the primitive *brujos* of Carlos Castaneda's landscape, whose secret knowledge of nature is the source of their powers. The potmakers of old are accomplices of nature. In making a pot, they wait for the right season, the correct time of day, choose the exact spot on the earth, the elevation, aridity, humidity. They check the turn of the wind, the colour of fire, and after attending to a hundred and one preparations, wait and pray for the unseen powers to favour the work of their alchemy.

I see the potter meditatively bent over the turning wheel, out of which rises a vessel of clay. That, I tell myself, is how I shall spend the days of my old age, turning out magical pots in some quiet retreat near the mountain or beside the sea.

Julie Lluch, Philippines

SETTING OUR FACES TO THE NEW JERUSALEM
(Luke 9:51-62)

"Jesus set his face to go to Jerusalem." In the set of his jaw, there was a sense of resoluteness. In his eyes there was an intensity – a clarity of vision – of purpose. He braced himself, picturing what was to come. And... gathering his courage, he prepared for the final act in the drama.

Jesus set his face to go to Jerusalem. Grounded in integrity, but with a sense of fear, even foreboding, Jesus lets the world see what he has known all along. On his face, in his message, he reveals the truth that he is the Messiah. In this moment, we have a sense of Jesus turning to face the reality of who he is.

This is a moment of transition – a moment when the interior becomes exterior. One... in a series of revelatory moments. In this moment Jesus faces rejection. His face, his message, his call – all are too bold, too extreme for the Samaritans who, we hear, "do not receive him because his face was set towards Jerusalem". We know that in Jerusalem he will face more than rejection: he will face his own death. We also know that rejection and death are not the whole story.

For lesbians, gay men, bisexuals, coming out requires a gathering of integrity. For many of us there is a sense of fear, even foreboding as we summon, invite and cajole the people we love to know us – as we let the world see the boldness of our faces, the many colours of our lives. In the moment – in fact, many moments – of transition, when the interior becomes exterior, we face rejection, sometimes subtle, sometimes harsh, sometimes brutal. In many countries of the world, being "out" means risking death. However, rejection and death are not the whole story.

After Jesus is rejected by the Samaritans he has an encounter with the disciples. Overwhelmed with a sense of their own power, they seek to bring fire down from heaven... Jesus rebukes them and just goes on with his journey, leaving the town behind. He then meets some potential followers. To each his response is less than sensitive. To a man who seeks to bury his father before following Jesus, he says, "Leave the dead to bury their own dead." To another wanting to say goodbye, he says, "No one who puts the hand to the plough and looks back is fit for the kingdom of heaven." This is the challenge of confident, committed discipleship – a warning that the road is difficult – no time for hesitancy, no turning back. This is not the comfortable pew, but a prickly prophetic message.

The challenge of the gospel to progressive communities of faith is the hard call to radical solidarity. We need to reveal more communities... who will wear both the pink triangle, the sign of oppression, and the rainbow, the sign of celebration and promise. How can churches who make this commitment support other churches who, acting in solidarity with gay and lesbian people, will go through their own coming out process, who will face, as we do, the rejection and alienation of the wider church? And who will risk leaving people behind? For those churches who accept the call, there is no turning back.

"Foxes have holes, and birds have their nests, but the Chosen One has nowhere to lay his head..." Jesus has no home, at least no home on earth. Perhaps because as Messiah he cannot be at home among oppressive systems, among wrong relations, where few live in the centre and many at the margins. Jesus' home is a world transformed, the new Jerusalem, the kingdom/community of God. We are invited to make that world a reality to achieve right relation, beyond hierarchies, beyond binaries. Neither slave nor free, male nor female, gay nor straight... We are invited to make a home for the risen Christ, who is both in us and outside us.

We set our faces to the new Jerusalem. We raise our voices in resolute commitment to justice. Our vision embraces diversity, our faces glow with the colours of the promise. We gather our own integrity, forging a strong empowered community, as we prepare the kingdom of God. Never turning back, never turning back.

Jennifer Henry, Canada

LOS QUE VIERON LA ESTRELLA

La Palabra se nos hizo pobreza en el
vestido del pobre, que vive del basurero.

La Palabra se nos hizo agonía, en el pecho
marchito de la mujer envejecida por la ausencia
del marido asesinado.

La Palabra se nos hizo sollozo mil veces apagado
en la boquita inerte del niño muerto por el hambre.

La Palabra se nos hizo rebeldía ante el cuerpo
inanimado de Gaspar Sánchez Toma, asesinado
por la "ciencia".

La Palabra se nos hizo peligro, en la angustia de
la madre que piensa en el hijo hecho hombre.

La Palabra se hizo ausencia siempre presente en
las 70.000 familias desgarradas por la muerte.

La Palabra se nos hizo acusación inexorable en
los cráteres ardientes que se tragaron sus
cuerpos torturados.

La palabra-cuchillo nos fustigó en el lugar de
la vergüenza, la verdad dolorosa de los pobres.

La Palabra sopló el Espíritu sobre los huesos
secos de las Iglesias-Momias, guardianas del
silencio...

La Palabra, clarín-de-madrugada, nos despertó
del letargo que nos robaba la Esperanza.

La Palabra se hizo camino en la selva, decisión
en el rancho, amor en la mujer, unidad en el obrero
y Estrella para unos cuantos sembradores de sueños.

La Palabra se hizo Luz,
La Palabra se hizo Historia,
La Palabra se hizo Conflicto,
La Palabra se hizo Espíritu Indomable,
y regó sus semillas
en la montaña
junto al río
y en el valle...

Y los *hombres-de-buena-voluntad*, oyeron el
canto de los ángeles.

Las rodillas cansadas se fortalecieron,
se afirmaron las manos temblorosas,
y el pueblo que vagaba en tinieblas,
vio la luz!

Entonces,
La Palabra se hizo carne en la *patria-prenada-
de libertad,*
En el Espíritu armó los brazos que forjaron la Esperanza,
El Verbo se hizo carne en el pueblo que vislumbra
un nuevo día...
Y se hizo vida en José y María que empuñan
el Derecho y sepultan la ignominia.

La Palabra se nos hizo *semilla-de justicia*
y concebimos la *paz.*

La Palabra gritó al mundo
la verdad de la lucha en contra del anti-hombre,
anti-mujer.

La palabra hizo llover la *justicia* y brotó *la paz*
en el surco de la tierra.

Y vimos su *gloria* en los ojos de los pobres
convertidos en hombres, en mujeres.

Y la Gracia y la Verdad se hicieron fiesta
en la risa de los niños rescatados por *la vida.*

Y, *los-que-vieron-la estrella*, nos abrieron el
camino, que ahora caminamos.

Mientras tanto, Herodes se va muriendo poco
a poco, comido de gusanos...

La Palabra se hizo juicio y los anti-hombres
rechinaron los dientes.

La Palabra se hizo perdón, y el corazón de
los hombres aprendió a palpitar el amor.

Y la Palabra seguirá sembrando futuros
en los surcos de la Esperanza.

Y, en el horizonte, La Palabra hecha luz, nos
invita a re-vivir mil madrugadas hacia el Reino que viene.

La Palabra nos convocará a su mesa.
Y vendrán del Este y del Oeste, del Norte
y del Sur, y vestidos de incorrupción,
estaremos-por-fin-alegres.

Julia Esquivel, Guatemala

THOSE WHO SAW THE STAR

The Word, for our sake, became poverty
clothed as the poor who live off the refuse heap.

The Word, for our sake, became agony
in the shrunken breast of the woman
grown old by the absence of her murdered husband.

The Word, for our sake, became a sob
a thousand times stifled
in the motionless mouth of the child
who died from hunger.

The Word, for our sake, became rebellion
before the lifeless body of Gaspar Sanchez Toma,
"scientifically" murdered.

The Word, for our sake, became danger
in the anguish of the mother
who worries about her son growing into
manhood.

The Word became an ever-present absence among
the 70,000 families torn apart by death.

The Word, for our sake, became an inexorable accusation
arising from the blazing craters
which swallowed up their tortured bodies.

The *word-knife* cut us deeply in that place of shame:
the painful reality of the poor.

The Word blew its spirit
over the dried bones of the Mummified-Churches,
guardians of silence.

The Word, that *early-morning-bugle*,
awoke us from the lethargy
which had robbed us of our Hope.

The World became a path in the jungle,
a decision on the farm,
love in women, unity among workers,
and a Star for those few who can inspire dreams.

The Word became Light,
The Word became History,
The Word became Conflict,
The Word became Indomitable Spirit,
and sowed its seeds
upon the mountain,
near the river
and in the valley...

And *those-of-good-will* heard the angels sing.

Tired knees were strengthened,
trembling hands were stilled,
and the people who wandered in darkness
saw the light!

Then,
The Word became flesh in a *nation-pregnant-with-freedom*,
The Spirit strengthened the arms which forged Hope,
The Verb became flesh
in the people who perceived
a new day...
And for our sake became life in Mary and Joseph
who embrace Righteousness and bury the people's ignominy.

The Word became the *seed-of-justice*
and we conceived *peace*.

The Word cried out to the world the truth
about the struggle against the anti-man, the anti-woman.

The Word made *justice* to rain
and peace came forth from the furrows in the land

And we saw *its glory* in the eyes of the poor
converted into true men and women.

Grace and Truth celebrated together in the laughter
of the children rescued by *life*.

And *those-who-saw-the star* opened up for us
the path we now follow.

Meanwhile, Herod slowly dying, is eaten by worms.

The Word became judgment
and the anti-humans ground their teeth.

The Word became forgiveness
and human hearts learned to beat with love.

And the Word shall continue sowing futures
in the furrows of Hope.

And on the horizon, the Word made light
invited us to relive a thousand dawns
towards the realm that comes.

The Word will gather us round her table,
And they will come from the East and the West,
from the North and the South,
and dressed in incorruption *we will-finally-be-happy*.

Julia Esquivel, Guatemala

THE SONG OF PEACE

THE SONG OF PEACE

The Song of Peace is a woman's song:
She sings the song of life's seasons –
rhythms of birth and death,
receiving and giving
times of waiting and fulfilment,
suffering and joy.

She sings a gentle song of *listening*
and *hope*
of *wholeness* and *unity*,
of *harmony* with the earth
and reverence for her gifts.

Her song is *compassion*
Her song is *love*.

If nations would be healed, *woman's*
song must be *sung*
If there would be peace, *woman's*
song must be heard.

Mary Southard, CSJ, USA

THE STORY OF WOMEN

The story of women and economic justice is a story of life and death

A story about endless agonies

A story about managing the unmanageable

A story of endless hours of work and toil

A story of sleepless nights

A story of hearing about destitution, squalor and neglect

A story of hearing about policies that determine our lives
        but never being there to participate

A story of the voiceless and the powerless

A story of trials and temptations

A story of lost personalities and dignity

A story of survival behind battle fronts
        as women and children flee bomb raids

A story of structural, emotional and physical violence

A story of struggle and humiliation

A story of dreams and visions unfulfilled

A story of hope

A story of withdrawal from structures of exploitation

A story of innovation and creativity

A story of breaking new frontiers for survival

A story of a heroic people marching to the future
        with new alternatives for the survival of the human race.

Agnes Chepkwony Abuom, Kenya

WOMEN MAKE THINGS GROW

Women make things grow:
sometimes like the crocus,
surprised by rain, emerging fully grown
from the belly of the earth;
others like the palm tree with
its promise postponed
rising in a slow
deliberate spiral to the sky...

Women make things...
and as we, in separate
worlds, braid
our daughters' hair
in the morning, you and I,
each
humming to herself, suddenly
stops
and hears the tune of the other.

Hanan Mikhail-Ashrawi, Palestine

THE SHARING

We told our stories
That's all.
We sat and listened to
Each Other
And heard the journeys
Of each soul.
We sat in silence
Entering each one's pain
And sharing each one's joy.
We heard love's longing
And the lonely reaching out
For love and affirmation.
We heard of dreams
Shattered.
And visions fled.
Of hopes and laughter
turned stale and dark.
We felt the pain of
Isolation and
The bitterness of death.

... And God's voice sang
In each story
Her life sprang from
Each death.

Our sharing became One Story
Of a simple lonely search
For life and hope and Oneness
In a world which sobs
For Love.
And we knew that in
Our Sharing God's voice with

Mighty breath
Was saying
Love each other and
Take each other's hand...

For you are one
Through many
And in each of you
I live.

So listen to my story
And share my pain
And death.

Oh listen to my story
And rise and live
With me.

Edwina Gately, Australia

EACH BIRD

Each bird
each one of us
bringing twigs
leaves
bits of blue plastic
whatevah!
to make a new nest
together
a leafy womb
enfolding our progeny
the ovum we will make together
born from our union
born from our struggle
born from communion.

Our leaves and twigs
made of heart
muscle and bone
Our song
born in ocean and weaned on struggle.
Strong clear voices
singing:
we have arrived!

We are here
we declare ourselves
we announce our presence
we tell our own stories...

Caroline Sinavaiana, Pacific

REGAINING THE "WE-NESS"

Look around you
     mountains, valleys, green grasses,
     flowers and trees...
Do you hear them beckon you
     to care, to nurture the creation?

People of all colours and ethnicity,
     the wonders of God's creation...
Do you feel the warmth,
     like the sun in the springtime?
Do you hear your heart beat
     like the calling of the drums?
Learning and knowing,
     you are not alone
     in the struggle to reclaim
     what is rightfully yours.

As I leave this place
     I bring with me...
the wisdom of our ancestors,
the resolve to make this world a place
     where children, families and communities
       are one with nature
       where justice, peace and sharing
       is a way of life.

I come with questions...
I am touched...
I leave with a smile!

Violeta Marasigan, USA

FROM THE DAWN OF TIME

Flying free
and flying blind sometimes
like Sarah walking the unknown
so many miles past Ur
But now
we walk without the tribe
except the ones
who tread the spaces in between
the past and future
with us.

And now and then
we turn around
to find the past has disappeared
or simply gone
from underneath
the place on which we stand
And life becomes
a sharp adventure
risky path
or simply one of faith.

The darkness has its outer edges
tinged with joy
of strength and newness
life and fullness
clouded round with grace.

And deep within the heart of us
we know our power to love
the centre of creativeness
which moves us on
beyond the named
and into worlds
which only we can claim
as ours.

If we will be and leap and dance
with life
to songs that always have
belonged to us
as women
from the dawn of time.

Dorothy McRae-McMahon, Australia

THROWING A STONE IN A CALM LAKE

A stone is thrown
into a calm lake
and the stone makes waves
spreading, reaching to the far end.

Let us throw stones
into a deadly calm lake
no matter how small is the stone
no matter how small is the wave.

The lake is like the world
The lake is like people's mind
The lake is like sisterhood
The lake is like human bondage
The lake is like chains of oppression

The stone brings awakening
The wave is a movement
And the movement spreads
when all of us
standing together on all sides
around the lake
keep throwing our little stones
The wave will never cease.

Till the whole lake
starts bubbling with life
Till the whole lake
makes its own spring
to keep its own life going.

Sun Ai Lee Park, Korea

WE ARE GOING HOME TO MANY WHO CANNOT READ

We are going home to many who cannot read,
so, Lord, make us to be Bibles,
so that those who cannot read the book
can read it in us.

by a Chinese woman
(after four months of Bible class
in which refugee women learned to read)

JESUS HEARD THE CRIES...

Jesus heard the cries of all the women he met
     and hears the cries of all women who weep now.
He acknowledges the context of personal and structural pain
     in which they were immersed.
Jesus gathers the tears of women and baptizes each one
     into a renewed and transformed life.
"If we were to gather together the tears already shed
     and as yet unshed by women around the world,
I believe we could baptize the church
     into a life of solidarity and resolute action."

Aruna Gnanadason, India

AFFIRMING COMMUNITY

We yearn for community. We seek it in our families, in our neighbourhoods, in our churches. We see in the Decade... a decade of possibilities when women and men can transcend all that divides and work towards becoming a concerned people. It is the brokenness of community that divides us.

It is the lack of community that creates economic injustice and makes poverty increasingly a women's issue. It is in our lack of community that racial injustice grows and that women under racism suffer the triple oppression of race, sex and poverty. It is our broken community that manifests itself in sexism, in oppressive structures that crush the spirit of women and also of men.

The creation of the full and true community, which is the aim of the Ecumenical Decade of Churches in Solidarity with Women, concerns all of us belonging to various churches, men and women; restoring the broken harmony of our communities we shall contribute to the transfiguration of the community as a whole... The Decade is a decade of hope and affirmation of community.

Olga Ganaba, Russia

RETHINKING THE CONCEPT OF PARTNERSHIP

A step forward in the SCM-WSCF experience is the rethinking of the whole concept of women-men partnership in concrete terms and situations. This must be built on a firm foundation, nurtured and sustained by a common understanding and perspective. This whole idea of a partnership is still more a rhetoric than a life-style. It is in fact an idea used by many people for different reasons, but far from instilling a commitment to genuine dialogue and the forging of a new relationship between men and women.

The idea of partnership implies an "open-ended" discovery of life together with new dimensions and dynamics. Since women's problems are men's problems, women's struggle for liberation should be equally men's struggle for liberation. This of course demands a loud and affirmative response from the men through discussion and study together. This also calls for a covenant between women and men to search and find out the true and meaningful partnership in their personal/individual lives and their collective life.

In the initial promotion of the women's programme, it was thought that only women needed liberation from all forms of gender oppression and violence; that women who struggled for their rights, for justice and freedom, had only to struggle for themselves and other women. The more progressive and enlightened men were only expected to assume their role and participation in terms of giving support and solidarity. But gradually, more and more women began to realize that men too need to be liberated from the claws of patriarchy in order that a new humanity can emerge – where both men and women can reflect the image of God that is in them.

The liberation of men is distinct from that of women. The former is perceived from the viewpoint of being the privileged group within a patriarchal ideology and system while the latter is the oppressed and discriminated group. And like women, men have to be freed from all this, beginning with the personal to the social, cultural and structural levels. But the thought of men's need for liberation is neither a widespread notion nor a realization by most men themselves. The process must start with a personal conviction and the commitment to change. Only then can responsible partnership come about and a total human liberation be possible.

Yong Ting Jin, Malaysia

MAKING SOLIDARITY REAL

In order to make their solidarity with women real, the churches should recognize the issues of women as justice issues and take them seriously. They should make every effort in their councils, synods and day-to-day ministry to understand the reality of these issues and not cast them aside as non-existent.

Let me give an example. A woman who is subject to domestic violence takes a long time to name it as such. Very often, we think something is wrong with us if things go wrong at home. It takes much courage to speak about it to a minister or an elder. Very often, after these steps have been taken, the woman is compelled to retreat into her corner again, because the church's response has been institutional; it does not discern the pain of the woman and fails to recognize the image of God distorted by her experience. The church fails to work to restore her human dignity. The ready response has always been to point out her marital vows to her.

All persons in ministry, ordained and lay, should be prepared adequately for a holistic ministry which encourages them to step into the shoes of others, to accept otherness and the richness of the diversity even when it threatens their own existence. If we can begin to do this, we will be working towards the discipleship of equals.

The role of the church in empowering women must also be one of a unifying presence – a presence which encourages women in the church – for instance in my part of the world – to begin to break caste, creed and race barriers. This process must address the tendency of universal patriarchal structures to divide women along the lines of race and class. It must address itself seriously to the need of women to build a global sisterhood and encourage this endeavour as beneficial to both church and society. This is done in war-torn Sri Lanka by women in church and society. Mothers and daughters of all classes, races and creeds work as sisters, and in one voice say No to war and opt for life, which is the very essence of the teaching of the four main living faiths in our country – Islam, Hinduism, Buddhism and Christianity.

Annathaie Abayasekera, Sri Lanka

A NEW WAY OF BEING

We women are not only the bearers of life. We are also the ones who care for life in all its manifestations; we bear the seeds of justice, equality, participation, dignity and life in all its abundance. That is why our actions are so intimately joined to the defence of life and the struggle against conditions that limit life, both in our churches and in global society.

This new vision cannot be divorced from a new attitude, a new way of being in the world and in history. If we accept God's message of salvation as integral and for all of human life, then it is impossible for us to separate reflection from action, rationality from feelings, commitment from celebration, or life from witness. This also means that we women must accept the fact of our womanhood as a possibility, a creative potential for personal development.

Our reflection encompasses our being, our body, our capacity for tenderness and struggle and all our particularities. This is what in Latin America we like to call the women's perspective, which has been enriching our theological and pastoral tasks for the last few decades. We are conscious that we form part of and contribute to a search for paths of liberation by a subjugated and overburdened continent.

This search is not a solitary one; neither is it merely sectoral. It is a common way, and its fruits are also shared communally; for as experiences are shared, a process of reflection and action is born. We have decided to be protagonists and participants in the daily battle against the forces of death, and this decision stems not from placid intellectual enquiry, but from the demands of our daily life.

As women, we encourage each other more and more to trust rather than compete, to build with others instead of looking for individualistic ways out, to share our fears and doubts in order to discover once again that in powerlessness, frailty and weakness, God's liberating power is manifesting itself.

About the element of celebration that we contribute in the construction of a new way of being church: it is the celebration centred in the triumph of Life over Death, which was the primary reason for the festive witness of women on the day of the resurrection. It is the joy shared among neighbours, like the woman who finds the lost coin. It is the celebration so often linked with surprises (as with Mary, the Samaritan woman and others), but it is also a celebration that motivates a witness not to be afraid to take risks.

This has been and continues to be a risky and challenging path, just like the risky and challenging march of our people, who from the standpoint of their faith want to participate in God's saving acts in history.

Nélida Ritchie, Argentina

MAGDALENE
DANCING IN CRIMSON

MAGDALENE DANCING IN CRIMSON

Mary Magdalene, who had been possessed by seven demons, recovered her whole personality after her encounter with Jesus. She followed him to the foot of the cross, even after the disciples had run away. She was the first person, even before Peter and John, to meet Jesus after his resurrection. She received his commission to love her neighbours as herself, as an expression of her love for him. In a resonance between the Bible and *Noh* drama, Magdalene dances and tells us of eternal love, among the maple leaves in crimson.

First scene (a moonlit night)

Chorus: *Maple leaves are dancing in crimson, maple leaves are dancing in crimson, the valley's heart will burn.*

Monk: I am a monk taking a look at all lands. I have arrived at God's city. Now, I mean to visit the hill of Golgotha. I am told this is the garden where Jesus died on the cross and was resurrected in three days. It is also here that someone who saw a wonder said, "Truly, this man was God's son!"

Mary: Where are you travelling to, you monks over there?

Monk: Are you speaking to me? Who and what are you, may I ask?

Mary: I am a woman living around here. The maple leaves scatter on the water, just like brocade. I live as a friend of the maple trees.

Monk: Indeed a friend of the maple trees is a friend of ours. We share a certain common fate, having the same heart.

Mary: We have met in this mountain path.

Monk: As friends.

Mary: Long ago, when I first met Jesus, I was a floating danger, possessed by seven devils. I wandered aimlessly, with my sleeves soaked with tears. One day Jesus regarded me and called me, "Mary, come to me." Touched by the light in his eyes, I turned away completely from the floating life of old. Since that day my sleeves are never so again. Since that day completely clean and fresh, my sleeves and myself.

Chorus: *In this world nothing is stable.*
Bearing the sins of the world,
he walked the way of sorrow to Golgotha.
His disciples ran away, but I followed him,
with his mother, to the foot of the cross.
The sinless son of God bore the sins of the world.
The sun hid in darkness.
At dark dawn I went to the tomb
to anoint the body of Jesus.
Who will roll away the large stone from the tomb?

Mary: But the large stone was rolled away,

Chorus: *and the body of Jesus was gone!*
How can I live if even his body is lost?

Jesus: Mary!

Chorus: *Jesus stood right behind Mary.*

Jesus: Why do you seek my love in the past? Is love not life after life? Love is forgiveness. Love is eternal. Love lives after death.

Mary & Jesus: Love is life after life. Love is forgiveness limitless.
Love is eternal. Love lives after death.

Monk: You seem to know Jesus in resurrection. Pray, say your name!

Mary: Actually I am the woman from the town of the tower, namely Mary Magdalene.

Chorus: *And also the first person who met Jesus in resurrection.*

Mary: How I love him.

Chorus: *The colour of love shows up in the maple leaves, which are also myself; thus she said, and hid herself in the rock.*

Second scene (the same night through the dawn)

Monk: I travel as far as the moon, I travel as far as the moon. As I wait for the dream I clear my mind like clearing the cloud. I clear my mind like clearing the cloud.

Chorus: *The white garment he left; shining so white, shining so bright.*

Mary: Is it my love that is calling my name?

Jesus: Mary, I have entrusted my hope to you.

Mary: Rabboni, show me the landmark of the realm of heaven.

Jesus: I no longer call you servant. You are my friend, as I have told you everything I heard from God.

Mary: How I love you, my love. Love is eternal.

Chorus: *My love, love is eternal.*
With you I overcome the stony path.
With friends I build the kingdom of heaven.

Jesus: Show your love to me by loving your neighbours as you love yourself.

Mary: I try to love my neighbours as I love myself. That is my love to you.

Chorus: *I love my neighbours as I love myself.*

Mary
and Jesus: Love is life even after life.

Chorus: *Love is forgiveness limitless.*
Love is eternal.
Life lives even after death.
Love is life eternal.
I shall be with you to the end of the world.
Let us walk towards the dawn.
Let us walk into the light of the kingdom of heaven.

Mary Magdalene dances in crimson

Chorus: *Swirling sleeves covered with maples.*
      I offer my sleeves to God.
      Maple leaves burn the heart of the valley crimson.
      Mary celebrates eternal love.
      The crimson maple is a symbol of eternal love in this transient world.
      Crimson is eternal love.

Yuko Yuasa, Japan

THE TABLE OF LIFE

Voice 1:   Come to the table
      where we can gather around close to the ground,
      where our roots find nourishment
      from the memory of our ancestors.

Voice 2:   How can we come to the table when we,
      indigenous peoples of the world,
      are uprooted from the land of our ancestors?
      In the name of development we are threatened.
      We have nowhere to go.
      Our land is mined and is barren.

Response: **Have mercy on us, Christ have mercy on us.**

Voice 3:   Come to the table
      to partake of the offering of our mothers
      whose love and warmth make the meal seem like a feast
      as we gather with joyful expectation.

Voice 4:   How can we come to the table
      when there are many mothers
      who are victims of violence against women?
      Many fear for their lives and their children, due to war;
      many have nothing to lay on their tables because of their poverty.

Response: **Have mercy on us, Christ have mercy on us.**

Reading

Then the word of the Lord came to him: "Go now to Zarephath, a village of Sidon, and stay there; I have commanded a widow there to feed you." So he went off to Zarephath. When he reached the entrance to the village, he saw a widow gathering sticks, and he called to her and said, "Please bring me a little water in a pitcher to drink." As she went to fetch it, he called after her, "Bring me, please, a piece of bread as well." But she said, "As the Lord your God lives, I have no food to sustain me, except a handful of flour in a jar and a little oil in a flask. Here I am, gathering two or three sticks to go and cook something for my son and myself before we die." "Never fear", said Elijah. "Go and do as you say; but first make me a small cake from what you have and bring it out to me; and after that make something for your son and for yourself. For this is the word of the Lord the God of Israel: 'The jar of flour shall not give out nor the flask of oil fail, until the Lord sends rain on the land'." She went and did as Elijah had said and there was food for him and for her and her family for a long time (1 Kings 17:8-15, NEB).

Reflection

Voice 5:   Come to the table
           Family, friends, strangers, street people,
           children, youth, adults, elderly,
           women, men, whoever you are,
           healthy and sick – everyone!
           Come and share in festivity.

Voice 6:   How can we come to the table
           When all around us we see
           separation, division, wars, domination?
           We are labelled.
           We do not belong.

Response: **Have mercy on us, Christ have mercy on us.**

Voice 7:   Come to the table.
           Let us serve one another,
           pass the food to your neighbour,
           participate in the feast of life.
           Come.

Voice 8:   How can we come to the table
           while there are those who are powerful
           and those who remain powerless?
           When there are those who are served
           and those who always have to serve?
           When there are those who tell others where to sit
           and keep the best places for themselves?

Response: **Have mercy on us, Christ have mercy on us.**

Reading

During supper Jesus took bread, and having said the blessing he broke it and gave it to the disciples with the words: "Take this and eat, this is my body." Then he took a cup and having offered thanks to God he gave it to them with the words: "Drink from it, all of you. For this is my blood, the blood of the covenant, shed for many for the forgiveness of sins" (Matthew 26:26-28).

Song

Prayer

Let us come to your table, loving Christ,
       mindful of our world,
       hearing the pains of your people
       and of your creation.

Let us come to your table,
       for hope in peace,
       for change in our ways,

for healing of pains,
for freedom,
for empowerment,
for life.

Silence

The Sharing

(Elements: a loaf of bread or rice cake, wine or juice or coconut water. A mother or woman takes the loaf of bread and offers it first to a child, who takes off a piece; the child then offers the loaf to another person until all have taken a piece of bread. When each has a piece, the mother or woman says, "Let us partake of the bread of life." A father may make the first offer of the cup and pass it on to an elderly person, and so on.)

Prayer of Thanksgiving

Song

Closing Prayer

Cora Tabing-Reyes, Philippines

THE WEB OF LIFE

Weaver-God, Creator, sets life on the loom,
Draws out threads of colour from primordial gloom.
Wise in designing, in the weaving deft:
    Love and justice joined – the fabric's warp and weft.

Called to be co-weavers, yet we break the thread
And may smash the shuttle and the loom, instead.
Careless and greedy, we deny by theft
    Love and justice joined – the fabric's warp and weft.

Weaver-God, great Spirit, may we see your face
Tapestried in trees, in waves and winds of space;
Tenderness teach us, lest we be bereft
    Of love and justice joined – the fabric's warp and weft.

Weavers we are called, yet woven too we're born,
For the web is seamless: if we tear, we're torn.
Gently may we live – that fragile Earth be left
    With love and justice joined – the fabric's warp and weft.

(Tune: Noel Nouvelet)

Kate Compston, England

Prayers

1.

Eternal God,

you have made us one people through the love of your Son,

you poured out your Spirit on us,

so that, renewed by your life-giving Spirit,

we may bring all our gifts that she brings to our common life.

In our quest for community

correct us where we have been wrong;

affirm us where we have followed your love;

renew us where we need to change our minds,

and strengthen us where faith calls us to new risks.

Loving God,

in all things keep us faithful to the message of your gospel,

that as women and men we may together bear witness

to that love which sets us free.

In Christ's name we pray. Amen.

2.

Listen to my prayer,

O God,

Do not ignore my plea

hear me and answer me.

My thoughts trouble me and I am distraught.

My heart is in anguish within me.

The terrors of death assault me.

Fear and trembling have overcome me.

If an enemy were insulting me,

      I could endure it.

If a foe were raising himself against me,

      I could hide from him.

But it is you, a man, my companion, my close friend

      with whom I once enjoyed sweet company,

      as we walked together in the house of God.

(From South Africa, author unknown. Taken from Women in God's Image, *No. 4, November 1997)*

3.

God of the poor,

come to us as a devout woman offering two mites.

God of the lost,

come to us as a prudent woman seeking a hidden coin.

God of the outsider,

come to us as an alien woman begging for crumbs off our table.

God of the sick,

come to us as a bleeding woman grasping for a healing touch.

God of the condemned,

come to us as a judged woman fallen before her accusers.

God of the hurt,

come to us as a beautiful woman washing our feet with her hair.

God of the dying,

come to us as a mourning woman grieving for her brother.

Compassionate God,

open our hearts to receive you

so that we may mark this day

as a time to recommit ourselves and our churches

to be in solidarity with women.

You have visited us through the women

who have been filled with your Spirit.

You have blessed us all with dreams for a common future

and gifts for a common life,

in all things keep us faithful to the message of your gospel,

that as women and men

we may together bear witness to your love in Christ Jesus. Amen.

MARY MAIDEN MOTHER

Mary maiden mother

Woman more womanly
in strength of surrender

You nurtured him
in your womb

You pondered him
in your heart

Reveal to me his presence

In the heart of every woman

Battered broken
struggling strong

Lead me into the womb
of the women's movement

Bursting into freedom strong

Judith Sequeira, India

LITANY OF MARY OF NAZARETH

Voice 1:   Glory to you, God our creator...
Voice 2:   Breathe into us new life, new meaning.

Voice 1:   Glory to you, God our Saviour...
Voice 2:   Lead us into the way of peace and justice.

Voice 1:   Glory to you, healing Spirit...
Voice 2:   Transform us to empower others.

All: **Be our guide.**

Voice 1:   Mary, wellspring of peace
             Model of strength
             Model of gentleness
             Model of trust
             Model of courage

Model of patience
Model of risk
Model of openness
Model of perseverance

All: Pray for us.

Voice 2:   Mother of the liberator
              Mother of the homeless
              Mother of the dying
              Mother of the nonviolent
              Widowed mother
              Unwed mother
              Mother of a political prisoner
              Mother of the condemned.

All: Lead us to life

Voice 1:   Oppressed woman
              Liberator of the oppressed
              Marginalized women
              Comforter of the afflicted
              Cause of our joy
              Sign of contradiction
              Breaker of bondage
              Political refugee
              Seeker of sanctuary
              First disciple
              Sharer in Christ's passion
              Seeker of God's will
              Witness to Christ's resurrection

All: Empower us.

Voice 2:   Woman of mercy
              Woman of faith
              Woman of contemplation
              Woman of vision
              Woman of wisdom and understanding
              Woman of grace and truth
              Woman, pregnant with hope
              Woman centred on God.

Author Unknown

EARTH CREDO

I believe in the sacredness of the earth,
the integrity of the whole creation and dignity of all peoples and creatures.

I believe in a gracious God
who created humankind, male and female, in God's image
and gave them the gift and responsibility to take care of the Earth.
We need to care.

I believe we human beings have failed God and ourselves.
In the name of greed and "development" we have dominated the earth,
degraded people and creatures,
destroyed the forests, polluted the air, rivers and seas,
and have sacrificed the future of our children.
We need to repent.

I believe that when we destroy the earth we kill ourselves.
We need to preserve and protect the earth,
not only for our own survival,
but for the sake of our Mother Earth.
The time to change is now.

I believe we need to change our ways, values, life-styles
and ways of relating with creation.
Repent, fast and pray. Consume less... waste not.
Work for justice and peace.
We should not covet our neighbours' timber, butterflies
    white beaches, nearly extinct animals nor cheap labour.
We should not oppress children, Indigenous Peoples, women
the homeless, refugees and victims of war.
We need to live in defence of people and creation.

For I believe in the inter-wovenness of life:
Creator and creatures... Breath and prayer
Cosmic and individual... Food and freedom
West, North, East, South...
Sexuality and spirituality
Ecology and theology

I therefore commit myself,
together with other concerned people everywhere,
to take care of Mother Earth,
to advocate for peace and justice,
to choose and celebrate life!
These things I believe. Amen.

Elizabeth S. Tapia, Philippines

MAYAN PRAYER

O God, beauty of the day, heart of the heavens and of the earth;
     giver of wealth, giver of daughters and of sons.
Help us to feel within ourselves the need to search for you,
to invoke your name, to praise you along the roads,
    in the valleys, in the ravines,
     on the riverbanks and under the trees.
Protect us, that we may not be entangled in evil,
     that we will not trip into shame and misfortune.
Help us not to slip and get hurt, that we may not fall along the way.
Protect us from obstacles that might pursue us or appear before us.
Give us only beautiful straight paths, beautiful good paths.
Grant that we might believe in you, be drawn to you
     and that our existence might be happy.
O God, heart of the heavens and of the earth, hidden treasure.
You fill the heavens and earth at the four cardinal points.
Grant that there might be only peace and tranquillity in the universe,
    before you, O God.
May it be so. Amen.

From the Popul Vuh

A PRAYER FOR LIFE

O God,
Source and fountain of life,
You are the Mother and Father of all living beings.
It is your essence within us we desire to touch;
we desire to receive blessings from your will and plan
for humanity and creation.

May we fulfill it with a relentless quest.
This day, let food be shared
    with all people of all nations.
Let justice and equality be lived by us.
Forgive us the times we have hoarded wealth
    and refused to share with others.
In moments of indifference to poverty, shake us.
In moments of temptation to dominate
    or to be sluggish, alert us.
Free us from a selfishness and fear,
make us grow in compassionate love
    so we can build a violence-free world
    in the communion of all persons and creation. Amen.

Author Unknown, India

A PRAYER

To the East,
> Which brings us the light of a new day,
> Wherein dwells inspiration and enlightenment,
> Thank you for this day and for your gifts.

To the South,
> Wherein dwells innocence and trust,
> From whence comes warmth, growth and new life,
> Thank you for this day and for your gifts.

To the West,
> Where the day ends,
> Wherein dwells darkness and introspection,
> From whence come the rains and the thunder begins,
> Thank you for this day and for your gifts.

To the North,
> Wherein dwells wisdom,
> From whence comes the cold,
> and the healing white blanket of winter,
> Thank you for this day and for your gifts.

To our Grandfather and Father above, The Sky,
> Wherein dwell all beings of air and light,
> Thank you for this day and for your gifts.

To our Grandmother and Mother at our feet,
> Who sustains us and provides us with all we need to survive,
> Thank you for this day and for your gifts.

We have abused them.
Have pity on us and help us walk in balance with you,
That we may return something of what we have taken.

To the Creator,
> Who is above and behind these and all things,
> Thank you for this day and for our lives.
> Thank you for the tools which you have given us.
> Teach us to use them well.
> Guide the seekers, that they may find what they are looking for,
> And understand.
> Help us heal ourselves, that we may heal others.
> Help us learn, that we may teach in our turn.

Take care of our Elders and keep them in health.
Their task is difficult,
As there are many of us and few of them.

Help us all come together as one people,
To complete and strengthen the great circle.
Help us live each day as a ceremony.
Meegwetch.

Author Unknown

A PRAYER FOR MOTHER EARTH

Blessed are you, O God,
    who gave me the gift of life,
    of breath, of a divine image in my woman's body.
Blessed are you, O Gracious and Compassionate Spirit,
    who provide wisdom and compassion
    to believing women and men,
    regardless of colour, creed, contexts and choices.
Fill the earth with love and peace, kindness and wholeness.
Fill my midlife years with passion and compassion,
    empty my heart of unhealthy emotions
    and fill it with energizing ones.
Lead me to the paths of righteousness, openness, justice,
    spirituality, sensuality and childlike joy!
Open my eyes to see the needy and the exploited,
    and when I see them, to be an advocate for them
    and to struggle with them.
Bless my dreams, hopes, passions; bless my body and mind as well.
Bless Mother Earth and all that is within her and around her.
You are Holy, O God,
You are One.
You are beyond me and within me.
Blessed be your name.
You created us human beings, male and female in your image.
As we celebrate life in the midst of life's uncertainty,
Bless our lives with shalom and genuine security.
    We are alive! We are struggling.
    We are hoping. We are women in midlife passion,
    With fire in our bellies and compassion deep within
      we can change the world.
    So be it.

Elizabeth S. Tapia, Philippines

ORACIÓN POR LA MUJER

Espíritu de Dios, hazla un instrumento de tu paz;
que donde haya división,
sea ella vínculo de unión,
que donde haya desconfianza,
pueda ella dar perdón,
que donde haya duda, ponga ella fe,
que donde haya tristeza, sea ella alegría,
que donde haya desaliento, sea ella
        camino de esperanza,
que donde haya sombras, sea ella tu luz.

Ella puede, porque le has dado
        un cuerpo de oblación,
        un vientre habitado de ritmo, música, tiempo y esperanza
        y una tarea de gozo y luz, de transfiguración.

Espíritu de Dios, derrama sobre ella,
tu Agua, tu Fuego, tu Brisa Suave, tu Vida Nueva,
Que reciba toda Sabiduría, de todas las culturas, plenamente
que desborde tu Fuerza Dulce y Suave
para construir con todo ser viviente
con toda su alma, sus energías, su corazón,
la Basilea de Justicia, Paz de toda la creación.
Hazla como Tú, Verdad, Libertad, Don
que habite como Tú, en el Río de Sangre, Agua
del Corazón del mundo.

Haz Espíritu de Dios, que vea en cada varón al hermano, al amigo, al hijo.
Haz Espíritu de Dios, que vea en cada mujer un pedazo de su propio ser.

Haz, que vea en la sociedad, la comunidad de personas a engendrar,
Haz, que su aspiración sea la imagen Perfecta, el Icono Total.

Hazla, un instrumento de tu paz.
Dale tu Espíritu de unidad, de concordia, de paz.
La tarea es inmensa: y su nombre verdadero es Jerusalén,
        la Santa, la del Cielo, Ciudad de Paz.

María Teresa Porcile Santiso, Uruguay

PRAYER OF THANKSGIVING
ON THE OCCASION OF THE YEAR OF
INDIGENOUS PEOPLES

God our Creator,
We thank you for our indigenous sisters,
their mothers and fathers,
sisters and brothers,
children, companions,
and all their ancestors, for Mother Earth
for their living respect
since immemorial times.

We give thanks, God,
for our indigenous sisters,
their resistance and courage,
in the endless struggle for life
overcoming centuries of destruction and death.

We give you thanks, God,
for our indigenous sisters,
their history shared with us,
their wisdom shared with us,
their hope shared with us,
making the links of our sisterhood stronger.

We also want to remember, our God,
all sisters around the world:
from north and south,
from west and east,
that they may be moved
by the wind of *Ruach*, the Spirit,
becoming living instruments
of healing in the world.

Amen.

Marilia Schüller, Brazil

A Prayer from Slovakia

Dear Heavenly Father,
I thank you from the depths of my heart
    for all the gifts and outpourings of your grace
    with which you bless us day by day.
Such a gift and expression of your grace
    was the Ecumenical Decade – Churches in Solidarity with Women.
I thank you that I was able to take part
    along with the women from other Christian churches
    in the opening worship service of the Decade in our country.
I thank you that I was able to host this opening worship service in
    my congregation.
The Decade has shown us many possibilities
    which we women should put to good use,
    with the help and support of our churches.
We thank you that in the Women's Association of our Evangelical
Church of the Augsburg Confession in Slovakia
    we now show more willingness to enter the service of love
    and to renew our diaconal activities.
We thank you that we could help a little, even though not very much, to bring
peace and protect creation.
Forgive us when we don't do enough to use the opportunities we have.
Forgive our church, we pray, when it doesn't use its opportunities
enough to support women working on Decade issues.
We don't want to stop now;
Let us go on with the work we have begun.
We pray to you, give the gifts of your Holy Spirit
    to our church leaders and to us – to all us women,
    so that in the work which we have begun
    we can win fathers, husbands, brothers and sons
    as partners in preserving peace, justice and creation,
    for the generations to come.
To you be thanks, honour and praise from us all,
    now and forever. Amen.

Darina Banzikova, Slovakia

BLESSINGS

1.

May you have a passion for justice when ours falters
May you have a sense of humour when we lose ours
May you have compassion for others when ours becomes selective
May you have strength and courage to risk when some of us are afraid
to speak up
Take us with you
Don't give up on us
You are the creators of the new.

Sr Marjorie Tuite, USA

2.

We will be together in these places.
We will watch out for each other.
We will listen to whatever needs to be said.
We will not be fearful or anxious or prodding when it seems
        that silence is the only possible response.
We will wait for the slowest.
We will sooner or later catch up with the fastest.
We will dry the tears of those who are weeping and know
        that they will dry ours when the time comes.
We will let ourselves begin to feel at least a little of the pain
        of those we have considered our enemies.
We will let ourselves feel the pain of being thought of as someone
else's enemy: not the pain of hurt feelings or of being
misunderstood, but the pain of acknowledging all those strands of
history that have put so many barriers between us.
We will not forget the joy of life; we will not forget to be grateful.
We will do our best to stir in each other the courage to act with
love and justice in our particular lives.

Mary Farrell Bednarowski, USA

HOLY WEEK MEDITATIONS

HOLY WEEK MEDITATIONS

From Monday to Thursday during Holy Week 1998, staff at the Ecumenical Centre in Geneva and friends gathered for a brief time of prayer, song and meditation. The year 1998 would mark the end of the Ecumenical Decade – Churches in Solidarity with Women (the Decade was launched at Easter of 1988); and the Ecumenical Centre worship team thus decided to focus on issues and struggles in which women around the world are engaged.

Each morning the community was invited to gather at a different location in the building as a way of focusing attention on where work in women's issues is being done in the various organizations which are part of the Ecumenical Centre family.

Scripture readings reflected the faithful discipleship of the women around Jesus.

For each liturgy a long piece of soft cloth (15 - 20 metres) was used in a symbolic way. At the conclusion of each meditation the cloth was draped around a plain wooden cross (2 metres high) and the participants joined in a procession to the place where they would gather the following morning. On Maundy Thursday, they walked with the cross to the open space outside the Main Hall of the Ecumenical Centre and left the cross there for the day. The cross and the cloth were then used again the next week for Easter worship.

MONDAY

CALL TO PRAYER

According to the ancient traditions of the church, when our Lord was carrying his cross his face could not be recognized because of the blood and sweat mixed with dust and dirt on it. Then a woman by the name of Veronica went forward, and with her handkerchief cleansed the face and made it possible once more for the real countenance to be seen. Men and women are made in God's image. God's face in them is so often unrecognized because of all kinds of dirt on them (Bishop Hassan Dehqani-Tafti, Iran).

Sometimes we forget that we are made in the image of God and we need a Veronica to wipe away all that keeps the face of Jesus from shining through. In this time of worship we are invited to gather around the large cloth. Imagine your face on the cloth. If you would like to, you are invited to touch the cloth or to put your face to it for a moment. In your face is there a reflection of the face of Jesus?

SONG

There are other faces on the cloth. Some have had the image of God blurred, marred or defaced by poverty or persecution, by worry or fear. These may be people far away from us, or our colleagues down the hall. What might the imprint of their faces ask of us? How might we lift their countenance? How might we carry a cross and wipe a face for the sake of the gospel?

PRAYERS OF INTERCESSION

Loving God,
We know that in many of our sisters and brothers
    your image has been scarred and tarnished.
They have been drained by exploitation.
Your image has been destroyed
    by people subjugating one another.
The female part of your image
    has been conveniently forgotten.
But you mean your creation to be good,
    your image to be whole.
Restore it, gracious God.

Loving God,
Be with the churches and people around the world,
    especially those who live in situations of violence or war,
    those who live in the shadows of struggle and despair.
Help us to live compassionate and justice-filled lives,
    so that each of us may see your image in one another.

PRAYER OF JESUS (THE LORD'S PRAYER)

SENDING FORTH

We will take with us the cloth of faces. As we follow the cross we take these faces with us. In the company of Veronica and Simon of Cyrene we are encouraged to assist Jesus, to assist those travelling with Jesus, to assist each other.

PROCESSION OF THE CROSS

SONG *May we see God's loving face*   Tricia Watts, Australia

DISMISSAL

TUESDAY

CALL TO PRAYER

SONG

GOSPEL READING   John 19:23-27

When the soldiers had crucified Jesus, they took his clothes and divided them into four parts, one for each soldier. They also took his tunic; now the tunic was seamless, woven in one piece from the top. So they said to one another, "Let us not tear it, but cast lots for it to see who will get it." This was to fulfill what the scripture says, "They divided my clothes among themselves, and for my clothing they cast lots." And that is what the soldiers did.

Meanwhile, standing near the cross of Jesus were his mother, and his mother's sister, Mary the wife of Clopas, and Mary Magdalene. When Jesus saw his mother and the disciple whom he loved standing beside her, he said to his mother, "Woman, here is your son." Then he said to the disciple, "Here is your mother." And from that hour the disciple took her into his own home.

REFLECTION ON THE WORD   Irja Askola

Even in the midst of cruel suffering, the powerful – the ones with guns and knives – are keen on benefitting from the situation. Let's take our share, let's get something out of this for ourselves. Like cloth, the human body can also be torn: they were ready to tear his body, but not the cloth. Let us not tear any material which could bring us some financial benefits! The hard faces of aggressive capitalism are present.

And as always, even there, where hard facts humiliate, isolate, violate and kill, there is always this word, "meanwhile" (v.25). Meanwhile – in addition to the witness of horrible facts and disgustingly inhuman behaviour – something else is happening as well. The consolation of the word "meanwhile" is that in the midst of the darkness and cruelty, there is another level to be seen, another interaction to be realized.

Through the text our eyes recognize four women standing nearby. For them, not only was the tunic seamless, but life was also seamless, not to be separated and segregated. In their understanding of life they simply had to stand nearby, to stay: "If we shared with him the hope and the healing, the joy and the growth, we will share with him this moment as well." The seamless life – not to be cut according to our pleasure, but to be shared as a whole. "If he has stayed with us, calling us out of the shadow, how can we leave him at the moment of this darkness?" They just stay; no words are needed. They feel the presence of one another and although it does not lower the pain, although their hearts are suffering with Jesus, they stay.

In so doing, they bring to us the strength of all those unknown and known women who do not flee but stay, even amid great suffering and pain to those they love. These invisible women, who in the midst of failures, frustrations and unnecessary suffering stay – they do not reject, do not run away. In these women the "meanwhile" comes true again. Even in the midst of cruel moments, when the hard realities hit, there is always another stream as well, for the word "meanwhile" calls us to hear, to see, to find those who share the pain, who do not run away.

And in another moment the silence is broken by a voice: Jesus speaks. Suddenly the divine part gives way to human gesture. The adult son in Jesus wakes when, from the cross, he looks at his earthly mother. He realizes that her life will be without any security after this. A lonely woman, the mother of a criminal sentenced to death. Human care takes over in this divine moment; tenderness fills the air. "My mother, my dear mother, she deserves somebody to take care of her." In the last moments of his life Jesus' earthly concern is to care for the future of a woman, to be concerned about her financial and social security. He organizes, in a way, her future, by making sure that she is not left alone.

Divine and human form a seamless tunic for him; in his life human and divine embrace each other. At the last moment he cares for a woman; and soon his first sentence as the Risen Christ will confirm his radical sensitivity: "Woman, why are you weeping?" (John 20:15). And the new community is born. Meanwhile, when the soldiers were casting lots for his cloth, in the midst of all this cruelty, John receives an invitation to emerge out of sadness and despair and see his new role. After all, in God's presence everything is about relationships. After all, it is about new relationships in which traditional barriers do not count. New mothers and new children find each other, over and over again, and the shared pain between those who do not run away will form a gate.

SONG

PRAYERS OF INTERCESSION

PRAYER OF JESUS (THE LORD'S PRAYER)

SENDING FORTH

> Your robe without seam
> It was your mother who wove it for you with her slim fingers,
> according to the art and skill and tradition of the ancestors.
>
> Weaving, she sang the songs of Judah,
> the song of Deborah, the song of Anna the prophetess,
> and the hymn of Miriam, sister of Moses.

Your robe without seam – look!
Along your arms, along your body it slips,
wrenched off by the executioners.
And you are the naked palm tree,
the palm tree shorn by the tempest;
you are the lone trunk without leaves, without branches,
without bark to shield you from the biting wind.

And you would die free and naked of the robe without seam,
naked of the tribal robe woven by your mother's fingers,
naked of the clan fervours that weave about the heart
like a nest of sympathy and pity.
And your mother is alone, and alone the beloved disciple
who trembles and feigns among the mob run riot,
and you are alone, and you are wholly love,
and you surrender yourself.

Lord Jesus, grant us to be naked and free
to give ourselves to your love,
that all who have become lonely through hate
find again in you
the brotherly, sisterly meeting place of all hearts.
Then your robe without seam
that your mother has woven with her slim fingers
shall become the gathering of all about you.

Author Unknown, Cameroon

PROCESSION WITH THE CROSS

SONG

DISMISSAL

WEDNESDAY

CALL TO PRAYER

SONG

GOSPEL READING   Luke 23:45-49

Then Jesus, crying with a loud voice, said, "Father, into your hands I commend my spirit." Having said this, he breathed his last. When the centurion saw what had taken place, he praised God and said, "Certainly this man was innocent." And when all the crowds who had gathered there for this spectacle saw what had taken place, they returned home, beating their breasts. But all his acquaintances, including the women who had followed him from Galilee, stood at a distance, watching these things.

REFLECTION   Ana Villanueva

"True, the elephant is stronger. But the ants... well, there are more of them" (from Adolfo Perez Esquivel, *Christ in a Poncho: Witness to the Nonviolent Struggle in Latin America*, Maryknoll, Orbis, 1983, p.13).

We are women. We are mothers. Our children have been taken away and we do not know where they are. Where were they taken? Where did they put them? Are they alive? Are they dead? *Where, where, where are they? We want to know, we need to know, we need to know!!!* Is there any grief as great as a bodiless burial? *Where is my child?*

And we started to ask, here and there. In hospitals and police stations, to the church and to the authorities. Nobody answers. *We need to know! Where are they? Where did they put them?* In our painful pilgrimage we started to recognize one another. We realized that we were not alone. This horror did not happen just to us. We were several, we were many, we were more and more. And each one of us, all of us had the same questions: *Where are they? Where did they put them?* No answer, but we did not give up. We went to Plaza de Mayo, the famous square where so many historical events related to our country took place. We carried the photos of our children, with their names and dates of disappearance. We stood in front of the presidential palace and shouted our anger and frustration. They were taken alive, we want them back alive!

The police came and threatened us: "You can't stand here! This is a public place, you are disturbing the way of the people! You can't shout here! You are disturbing the peace!" They pushed us, they shouted at us. These were voices without eyes. They did not see, they did not want to see that we were demanding the lives of our children. We could not keep silent, we could not stop searching. But since we were not allowed to stand there and shout our rage and pain, we started to walk in silence two by two around the square. And our silence became our loudest cry. Our presence could not be ignored. We were there to be witnesses of the horror that eats away at society, and in spite of it to make a claim for life in the midst of death. We would never give up the hope of finding out what happened to our children. We would never abandon our children and their memory. We will never stop demanding justice! We did not speak, but our voices were heard all over the world and more and more people joined us.

"Mad women of Plaza de Mayo" we were called. Mad women, indeed, but with the madness of ants attacking the elephant of brute force. With the obduracy of a mother's love in a desperate appeal to whatever human sensitivity might still be in the heart of a despot. With the courage of defenceless women – some are missing now themselves – silently holding up a name or a photograph before the downtown crowd: "Where is my child?"

We are women who had known only how to love their dear ones; now suddenly we know why these dear ones are suffering, and how we ourselves must accompany them on the road of suffering! The way will be long, but not fruitless.

And we look to tomorrow. We know that much remains to be done. But we still have hope. Now that we know we are not alone, we have an expectation to which we can cling until such time as the storm is weathered and we have achieved a definitive, satisfactory solution. For tomorrow is what we make it, and it will be ours. (*Christ in a Poncho*, pp.45-46).

When Jesus was crucified, there was a crowd around; and his acquaintances, including the women who had followed him from Galilee, stood at a distance watching. They did not run away. The text does not put words in their mouth, but they were there; they were afraid, but they witnessed the horror, they accompanied their beloved one and defied the powerful with their presence. They expressed their resistance by being together and not giving up, in the middle of death. Let us remember all those women and men all over the world who, even without spoken words today, still shout out for justice and stand by the oppressed, aware that there are other Christs, the victims of new crucifixions.

HYMN   *Cancion de Caminantes*   Maria Elena Walsh, Argentina

PRAYERS OF INTERCESSION

(During intercessions, photos of the Mothers of Plaza de Mayo are laid on the cloth)

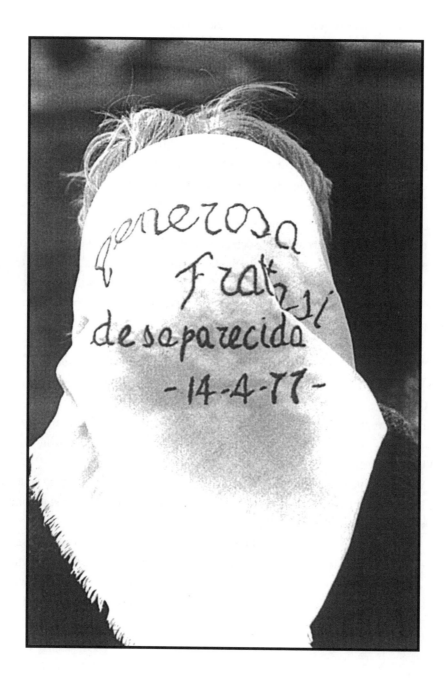

PRAYER OF JESUS (THE LORD'S PRAYER)

SENDING FORTH

> I am no longer afraid of death;
> I know well
> its dark and cold corridors
> leading to life.
>
> I am afraid rather of that life
> which does not come out of death
> which cramps our hands
> and retards our march.
>
> I am afraid of my fear
> and even more of the fear of others,
> who do not know where they are going,
> who continue clinging
> to what they consider to be life
> which we know to be death!
>
> I live each day to kill death;
> I die each day to beget life,
> and in this dying unto death,
> I die a thousand times
> and am reborn another thousand
> through that love
> from my People,
> which nourishes hope!
>
> *Julia Esquivel, Guatemala*

PROCESSION WITH THE CROSS

SONG

DISMISSAL

MAUNDY THURSDAY

SILENCE

CALL TO GATHER

L: God, O that you would tear open the heavens and come down,

C: **At that moment the curtain of the temple was torn in two from top to bottom,**

L: O that you would tear open the heavens and come down, so that the mountains would quake at your presence.

C: **At that moment the curtain of the temple was torn in two from top to bottom, the earth shook and the rocks were split!**

L: O that you would tear open the heavens and come down, so that the nations might tremble at your presence.

C: **At that moment the curtain of the temple was torn in two from top to bottom; the tombs were opened and many of the bodies of the saints that had fallen asleep were raised.**

HYMN *My Beloved, where can I find you?*   Jordan, Palestine, Lebanon, Syria

A PRAYER

God of all time and space,
We come before you in prayer.
In many countries, women wear the veil as a sign of identity,
        as a sign of self-worth, as a mark of integrity.
But it is not always so...
Just when lost and shattered dreams, when suffering and despair
        are uncovered and exposed – a new place is revealed
        where confidence and hope begin to grow –
And the veil is torn...
(part of the cloth-veil is torn)

In many countries, women wear the veil when they marry,
        as a sign of covenant and rejoicing.
But it is not always so...
Just when complicity through silence is no longer concealed –
Old systems and structures begin to be torn
        by God's promise of freedom and love for all.
And the veil is torn...
(part of the cloth-veil is torn)

When women give birth,
the veil of flesh covering the womb is torn,
        so that new life may come with hope and delight.
But it is not always so...
Just when we work to resist the assault on those whose lives,
        or whose children's lives are broken from lack of strength
        and hope –
God's power – midwife of our lives – creates a new space
        whose truth and peace are nourished and sustained.
And the veil is torn...
(part of the cloth-veil is torn)

In many countries, the veil is worn
as a symbol of dedicated lives,
as a reminder of God's peace and God's promise.
But it is not always so...
Just when the promise of new life is hidden
        from those who know only struggle and despair –
Then we, and all your people, God,
commit ourselves to the breaking down
of old traditions and systems –
so that the veil of all

that goes against your covenant with all of creation,
 shall be torn in two, from top to bottom...
(part of the cloth-veil is torn)
Amen.

GOSPEL READING   Luke 23:44, 49-56

It was about noon, and darkness came over the whole land until three in the afternoon, while the sun's light failed; and the curtain of the temple was torn in two.

And all his acquaintances, including the women who had followed him from Galilee, stood at a distance, watching these things. Now there was a good and righteous man named Joseph, who, though a member of the council, had not agreed to their plan and action. He came from the Jewish town of Arimathea, and he was waiting expectantly for the kingdom of God. This man went to Pilate and asked for the body of Jesus. Then he took it down, wrapped it in a linen cloth, and laid it in a rock-hewn tomb where no one had ever been laid.

It was the day of Preparation, and the sabbath was beginning. The women who had come with him from Galilee followed, and they saw the tomb and how his body was laid. Then they returned, and prepared spices and ointments. On the sabbath they rested according to the commandment.

REFLECTION ON THE WORD   Aruna Gnanadason
                                                   Mark 23: 49-56

And they saw the tomb and how the body was laid. In other versions of the Bible the phrase "they saw the tomb" is translated as "they marked the place where the tomb was".

Such a small detail, noticing where the body was laid, but it was important to the women. After preparing the spices and ointments they rested the next day, as it was the sabbath, the Bible tells us. Such a small detail... but so important.

Such small details the gospel writers record and these texts have accompanied us during this week... the women who were part of the crowd, the woman who wiped the blood and sweat from Jesus' face, the women who stood at a distance and just watched helplessly, the women at the foot of the cross... and today in the reading the women who marked the place where the body was laid. Throughout this week we have remembered these women – their faith and faithfulness, their compassion, their own personal pain and loss. It was important to remember these women, the faithfulness of all women everywhere, who wait patiently, who mark the graves of their sons, their husbands, their brothers, their grandchildren. Women who silently suffer in abusive relationships, perhaps marking their own graves?

Women who marked the graves of their children... In 1799, 32-year old Martha Marshman from England accompanied her husband Joshua Marshman as a Baptist "missionary wife" to Serampore, India. Leaving behind her country and family, she ventured into a strange new world in obedience to the call her husband received to go to India as a missionary and there to engage in educational ministries. Martha became the "mother of Serampore", sometimes feeding up to 60 orphans and children of other missionaries and at the same time running several schools. She was herself the mother of eight children, four of whom died of disease. Of this tragedy she is recorded to have said, "God has given me eight children, taken four of them to himself and allows me the other four for a certain time – how long is known only to him." Such faithfulness, such overwhelming faith. They have marked the graves of their children...

Such wrenching pain Mary must have felt as she watched them crucify her son... Did she have a choice? Was her needless pain justified? The mother of Ken Saro Wiwa, of Steve Biko, of the child soldier in one of the wars in many parts of the world. The mother of the child abused by a clergyman in a Christian boarding school, the mother who sends her child into prostitution because of poverty... the mothers who watch their children die of malnourishment, who watch their young daughters writhe in pain under the knife in female genital mutilation... Do any of these mothers have a choice? Is their needless pain justified?

Such wrenching pain... the Body is torn apart by insolent might, their bodies are torn by their grief, and the curtain is torn in the midst of thunder and the trembling of the whole earth. Feel these various emotions for just a moment. There is a purpose... there is the resurrection to move towards... there is hope, there is life, there is love.

They marked the place where the body of the Saviour was laid... It all had a purpose. It was in preparation for the Easter morning sunshine of hope, when these myrrh-bearing women would go to the tomb they had marked to anoint the body of their beloved, and find the tomb empty.

It was important to remember all these women during this week – women all over the world, who in this season will remember that ten years ago the churches had also embarked on a journey of faithfulness with women – the Ecumenical Decade of the Churches in Solidarity with Women. This Decade is ending, but the love of women for the church, their faith and faithfulness endures, their deep hope in the resurrection promise sustains them.

And so we go into this Maundy Thursday to drink and eat with our Saviour – a last supper, before the cruel pain and senseless suffering of the cross. As men and women, as the church, we eat and drink again and again, with our Saviour, his body and his blood – to commemorate, with hearts full of thanks, this remarkable love.

The earth shakes, the heavens thunder, the curtain is rent asunder... but the women with patient endurance and remarkable tenderness mark the tomb where the body will be laid.

S O N G

P R A Y E R S   O F   T H E   P E O P L E

P R A Y E R   O F   J E S U S   (T H E   L O R D ' S   P R A Y E R)

S E N D I N G   F O R T H

> Not straight away. Not at once.
> Not in the moment of time in which the veil was torn in two.
> Not immediately in order to comfort and promptly
> to assure his stricken friends,
> his ravaged mother, the sorrowful women.
> No.
> He did not rise at once. But on the third day.
> It was only when the fact of death had arrived
> at successively deeper levels into the friends' minds;
>> when information had become knowledge,
>> when knowledge had become truth,
>> when all were quite sure he was dead:

It was only then that he rose again.

Lord, when we wait for your promises to come true,
give us patience, give us faith, give us hope, give us obedience
to wait for the "third day".

PROCESSION WITH THE CROSS

SONG

DISMISSAL

L: We go forth from this time and space
in the name of Jesus, the Christ
who was broken to heal the world,
in whose death lies the secret of all life
and the hopes of all people.
God in Christ, we are with you, be with us now and always.

C: **And may the blessing of the God of Sarah, Hagar and Abraham,
the blessing of the Son, born of Mary;
The blessing of the Holy Spirit who broods over us
as a mother over her children, be with us all. Amen.**

SONGS

ALL ACROSS THE NATION, ALL AROUND THE WORLD

African Women's Day song

All a-cross the na-tion, all a-round the world wo-men are long-ing to be free. No lon-ger in the sha-dow forced to stay be-hind, but side by side in true e-qua-li-ty. So sing a song for wo-men e-very-where let it ring a-round and nev-er, nev-er cease. So sing a song for wo-men e-very-where: E-qua-li-ty, de-ve-lop-ment and peace.

ASATO MA SADGAMAYA

Lento and very free

India

1st time Leader   2nd time People

A-sa-to ma sad-ga-ma-ya Ta-ma-so ma jyothir-ga-ma-ya

Mri-tyor ma am-ri-tam ga-ma-ya.

Lead me from the unreal to the real, from darkness to light, from death to deathlessness.

AYYUHAL MASSLUBU ZULMAN

Arabic

Jordan, Palestine, Lebanon, Syria

1. Ay-yu- hal mass-lu-bu zul-man ya-mu-na qal-bil-ka-ïb. Ka-bi-
1. So much wrong, a great in-jus-tice, for you had to bear the cross. All my
1. Gros-ses Un-recht ist ge-sche-hen, weil das Kreuz du lei-den mußt. Mei-ne

di-har-rah wa qual-bi 'a-li-qon fau-qas-sa-lib. Wa ha-
dreams are lost and shat-tered, my heart hangs, too on the cross. My be-
Träu-me sind ver-lo-ren, und mein Herz hängt mit am Kreuz. Du Ge-

Refrain

bi-bi wa ha-bi-bi-ay-yu ha-len an-ta fih, dzuq-ta
lo-ved, my be-lo-ved, tell me: where can I find you? You who
lieb-ter, du Ge-lieb-ter, sag, wo fin-de ich dich nun, hast den

ka'-sal-mau-ti kai-ma yah-ya sha'-bon taf-ta-dih.
drank the cup of suf-fer-ing that your peo-ple might have life.
To-des-kelch ge-trun-ken, da-mit dein Volk le-ben kann.

2. Shajaru z-zaïtuni yahnu
bakian Rabba-l-Galal.
Wa tanuhu-l-Qudsu huznan
watulabbiha-l-gibal.

2. Olive trees were also crying,
they were grieving for their Lord.
And Jerusalem was mourning,
hills and mountains crying, too.

2. Die Olivenbäume weinten,
trauerten um ihren Herrn.
Und Jerusalem war traurig,
seine Berge weinten mit.

3. Ya habibi ayyu lahnen
min shaja-l-qalbi-l-hazin
yamnahu-r-ruha 'aza'an
wa yusalli-l-mu'minin.

3. There is no song and no tune
which can heal my broken heart.
Not alone I must be grieving,
all believers suffer, too.

3. Es gibt keine Melodie,
die trösten kann mein wundes Herz.
Nicht nur ich allein muß trauern,
alle Gläub'gen leiden mit.

Arabic © Jubrail Gabbour. English © Jeffrey T. Myers. Deutsch Dieter Trautwein, © Strube Verlag, München.

DON'T TELL ME OF A FAITH THAT FEARS TO FACE THE WORLD AROUND

Iona Community: Scotland

1. Don't tell me of a faith that fears to face the world a-round; don't
2. Don't speak of pi-e-ty and prayers di-vorced from hu-man need; don't
3. Don't save my soul with com-mon sense dis-tilled from a-ges past, in-
4. Don't set the cross be-fore my eyes un-less you tell the truth of
5. So let the Gos-pel come a-live in ac-tions plain to see, in

dull my mind with fick-le thoughts of grace with-out a ground.
talk of spi-rit with-out flesh like har-vest with-out seed.
ept for those who fear the world's a-bout to breathe its last.
how the Lord who finds the lost was of-ten found un-couth.
im-i-ta-tion of the one whose love ex-tends to me.

I need to see that God is real, I need to know that Christ can feel the
I need to know that Christ can feel.

need to touch and love and heal the world, in-clu-ding me.

© 1998, 1997 WGRG, Iona Community, Glasgow G51 3UU, Scotland

FOR SUCH A TIME AS THIS

Esther 4:14

Laveta Hilton: USA

♩ = 126

For such a time as this, we are called to com-
mit-ment, for such a time as this we are called to the
strug-gle. sometimes to lis-ten, sometimes to weep,
sometimes to risk or to speak. Called to be car-ing
called to act, for such a time as this.

In ei-ner Zeit wie jetzt ha-ben wir uns ver-
pflich-tet. In ei-ner Zeit wie jetzt dür-fen wir nicht mehr
zö-gern: manch-mal zu re-den, manch-mal zu schrein,
manch-mal ris-kie-ren zu kämpfen; sol-len wir sor-gen,
handeln und gehn, in ei-ner Zeit wie jetzt.

En ce temps au-jourd'-hui, ap-pe-lées à l'en-
gage-ment, en ce temps au-jourd'-hui, ap-pe-lées au
com-bat. Par-fois pour é-cou-ter ou pour pleu-rer,
par-fois pour risquer ou pour parler, appe-lées à en-tourer
ou à a-gir. En ce temps au-jourd'-hui.

En tiem-po co-mo e-ste, lla-ma-das al com-pro-
mis-o, en tiem-po co-mo e-ste, lla-ma-das a la
lu-cha. A ve-ces a es-cu-char. A ve-ces a llo-rar,
veces a arries-gar nos a hab-lar, llama-das a ser-vir,
llamadas a ac-tuar, en tiem-po co-mo e-ste.

© 1990 Laveta Hilton, 4162 Cimarron Drive, Clarkston, GA 30021, USA.

GIB MIR DEINE HAND

Uwe Seidel

Fritz Baltruweit: Germany

All rights by © Dagmar Kamenzky, Musikverlag, Hamburg, Germany. English, Irmgard Kindt-Siegwalt adapted. Spanish, Pablo Sosa.

HOW CAN WE STAND TOGETHER

Iona Community: Scotland

Traditional: England

1. How can we stand to-geth-er if we don't ag-ree to meet? Why
2. 'Stand up' says God and see the crime which sub-tly stalks the land. In-
3. The sound of emp-ty praise and prayer which drowns the cries of need; the
4. Be-cause he came a-mong us, washed our feet and broke our bread; be-
5. So let us stand to-geth-er as in Je-sus' name we meet. No

should we walk in cir-cles if no fet-ters bind our feet? How
te-gri-ty is not a word the pow-er-ful un-der-stand. The
mas-que-rade of cha-ri-ty which cov-ers up for greed; the
cause he sat with beg-gars, and en-sured that all were fed; be-
lon-ger tread-ing cir-cles, we'll walk close be-hind his feet. Nor

dare we talk of los-ing when de-feat is far from sure? How
man-sions of the rich are blessed by state and si-ne-cure. And
lust to do what's prop-er these are things I can't en-dure. Shall
cause he dared to break the law and cursed wealth's con-stant lure, we
shall we talk of los-ing since the faith-ful-ness is sure of

can the Lord be neu-tral when the priv-ileged fleece the poor?
shall the Lord be neu-tral when the priv-ileged fleece the poor?
I, the Lord, be neu-tral when the priv-ileged fleece the poor?
see God can't be neu-tral when the priv-ilged fleece the poor?
Christ, the King of Hea-ven and the Sav-iour of the Poor.

Words and arrangement © 1990, 1997 WGRG, Iona Community, Glasgow, G51 3UU, Scotland.

LA BENDICIÓN DE DIOS DE SARA, AGAR Y ABRAHAM

Pablo Sosa: Argentina

La ben-di-ción de Dios de Sa-ra, A-gar y A-braham, la ben-di-ción del Hi-jo que
The bless-ing of the God of Ab-ra-ham and Sarah, the bless-ing of the Son,

de Ma-ría na-ció, la ben-di-ción del San-to Es-pí-ri-tu de a-mor, que ve-la por no-
born of Ma-ry, the bless-ing of the Ho-ly Spi-rit, who in love is brood-ing ov-er

so-tros cual ma-dre por sus hi-jos, des-cien-da so-bre us-te-des. A-mén.
us as a moth-er o'er her chil-dren, be with us all for-ev-er. A-men.

Melody and Spanish, © Pablo Sosa, Buenos Aires, Argentina. The Spanish was a translation of a benediction by Lois Miller, Canada.

LET MY PRAYER RISE BEFORE YOU AS INCENSE

Psalm 141:2

I-to Loh: Taiwan

Let my prayer rise be-fore you as in-cense, the lift-ing
prayer

up of my hands as an even-ing sac-ri-fice.
up   sac-ri-fice.

© 1990 I-to Loh, Tainan Theological Seminary, 117 Section 1, Tung Men Road, Tainan, Taiwan.

LOVE JOJK

Traditional jojk as taught by Anna Åkerlund: Sweden

Jojk is traditional Sami singing. A Sami person would use a jojk to sing a subject and not to sing about it. Since this is a love jojk, love itself is being sung. The melody itself carries the theme. Some jojks can have a text to accompany the melody but most of them - such as this one - use non-sense words such as "Ha-le-la-e" or "Le-o-lo-la". This jojk can be sung as a canon.

MAY THE BLESSING OF GOD GO BEFORE YOU

Miriam Therese Winter: USA

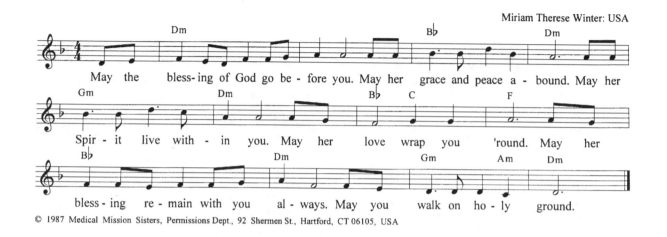

May the bless-ing of God go be-fore you. May her grace and peace a-bound. May her
Spir-it live with-in you. May her love wrap you 'round. May her
bless-ing re-main with you al-ways. May you walk on ho-ly ground.

© 1987 Medical Mission Sisters, Permissions Dept., 92 Shermen St., Hartford, CT 06105, USA

MAY WE SEE CHRIST'S LOVING FACE

Trisha Watts: Australia

May we see Christ's lov-ing face. May we be an i-con of his grace.

© 1992 Trisha Watts, Willow Connection Pty. Ltd., PO Box 341, Dee Why, NSW 2099 Australia.

OUVE DEUS DE AMOR

Simei Monteiro

Melodia Guaicuru adap. Simei Monteiro

Ou-ve Deus de a-mor nos-so cla-mor! Ou-ve Deus de a-mor
nos-so cla-mor! Ou-ve Deus de a-mor, Ou-ve Deus de a-mor,
Ou-ve Deus de a-mor, Ou-ve Deus de a-mor, O nos-so cla-mor, O nos-
so cla-mor, Ou-ve Deus de a-mor nos-so cla-mor!

Melodia coletada, 1945. The melody is based on a Native Brazilian tune. It is accompanied by a shaker.

¡Oye Dios de amor nuestro clamor! *Oh Lord, hear our cry!*

PORQUE EL CAMINO ES ÁRIDO

Maria Elena Walsh: Argentina

1. Por-que el ca - mi - no es á - ri - do y de - sa - lien - ta,
2. Si por de - li - ca - de - za per - dí mi vi - da,
3. Á - ni - mo nos da - re - mos a ca - da pa - so,
4. Por - que la vi - da es po - ca, la muer - te mu - cha,

por - que te - ne - mos mie - do de an - dar a tien - tas
quie - ro ga - nar la tu - ya por de - ci - di - da,
á - ni - mo com - par - tien - do la sed y el va - so,
por - que no hay guer - ra pe - ro si - gue la lu - cha,

por - que es - pe - ran - do a so - las po - co se al - can - za,
por - que el si - len - cio es cruel, pe - li - gro - so el via - je,
á - ni - mo, que aun - que ha - ya - mos en - ve - je - ci - do,
siem - pre nos se - pa - ra - ron los que do - mi - nan,

va - len más dos te - mo - res que u - na es - pe - ran - za.
yo te doy mi can - ción, tú me das co - ra - je.
siem - pre el do - lor pa - re - ce re - cién na - ci - do.
pe - ro sa - be - mos hoy que e - so se ter - mi - na.

¡Da - me la ma - no y va - mos ya! ¡Da - me la ma - no y va - mos ya!

1. *Because the road is rough and discouraging*
Because we are afraid of feeling our way in the darkness
Because waiting alone one gains very little
Two fears have more power than one hope

Chorus:
Give me your hand and let's go now

2. *If I lost my life through carefulness,*
I want to gain yours through action
Because silence is cruel and the journey is dangerous
I give you my song, and you give me courage.

Chorus

3. *We will encourage each other step by step*
Encourage each other as we share thirst and drink
Encourage each other because even as we get older
Pain seems always to be newly born.

Chorus

4. *Because life is short and there is much death*
Because there is no war but the struggle continues
We were always separated by those who dominate
But we know today that this has an end.

Chorus

LE LO LE LO LAY LO

William Loperena O.P.: Puerto Rico

Pronunciation in English is "Lay, loh, lay, loh, lay, loh, lye, loh" etc.

SHALOM, SAWIDI, A PAZ

From "Missa da Terra Sem Males"

D. Pedro Casaldáliga, Pedro Tierra,
Martin Coplas: Guarany, Brazil-Paraguay

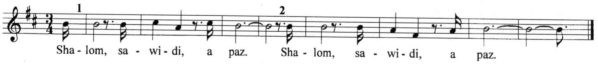

Peace, Friede, Paix, Paz, Pace

SHE COMES SAILING ON THE WIND

Gordon Light: Canada

Refrain

She comes sail-ing on the wind, her wings flash-ing in the sun; on a jour-ney just be-
Sur ses ai - les dé-ploy-ées au - ré - o-lées de so - leil el-le prend son en-vo-
Sie kommt se-gelnd mit dem Wind, in der Son - ne leuch-tet sie, ih-re Rei - se nimmt sie

gun, she flies on.   And in the pas-sage of her flight, her song rings out thro' the
lée dans le vent.   Et au sein de l'obs-cu-ri - té son chant fait vi-brer la
auf durch die Welt.   Und ihr Ge-sang tönt in der Nacht, Licht und La-chen bringt sie

night, full of laugh-ter, full of light, she flies on.   1. Si - lent wat-ers
nuit plein de ri - res et de lu-mière dans le vent.   1. Et les eaux se
mit, auf der Rei - se, die be-ginnt durch die Welt.   1. Wie die lee - re

Verse

rock-ing on the morn-ing of our birth, like an emp-ty cra-dle wait-ing to be
ber-cent à l'au-be du pre-mier jour com-me un ber-ceau vide pa - ré pour la
Wie - ge war-tet auf un-sre Ge-burt, wie die ru-hige Wo-ge schau-kelt auf dem

filled, to be filled. And from the heart of God the Spir-it moved up-on the earth, like a
vie, pour la vie. Et du coeur de Dieu l'Es-prit se ré-pand sur la terre en - tière u - ne
Meer;   und wie bei ei - ner Mut-ter, die dem Kind das Le-ben schenkt, kam der

moth - er breath - ing life in - to her child.
mè - re souf - flant vie dans son en - fant.
Geist aus Got - tes Her - zen in die Welt.

2. Many were the dreamers whose eyes were given sight,
When the Spirit filled their dreams with life and form.
The deserts turned to gardens, broken hearts found new delight,
And then down the ages still she flew on.

3. (To a) gentle girl from Galilee, a gentle breeze she came,
A whisper softly calling in the dark,
The promise of a child of Peace, whose reign would never end,
Mary sang the Spirit song within her heart.

4. Flying to the river, She waited circling high,
A-bove the child now grown so full of grace.
As he rose up from the water, She swept down from the sky,
And She carried him away in her embrace.

5. (Long) after the deep darkness, that fell upon the world,
After dawn return'd in flame of rising sun.
The Spirit touched the earth again, again her wings unfurled,
Bringing life in wind and fire as She flew on.

2. Nombreux sont les rêveurs qui ont retrouvé leur vie
quand l'Esprit aux rêves donna forme et vie.
Les déserts sont refleuris,
les coeurs brisés retrouvent joie.
La colombe reprend son vol dans le temps.

3. Et la douce brise caressa la jeune fille
un murmure dans la nuit de son destin.
Une promesse de paix dans un enfant au règne sans fin.
Et le coeur de Marie déborda de chants.

4. La blanche colombe vers le Jourdain prit son vol
et plana sur le jeune homme plein de grâce
et descendit sur lui qui sortait de l'eau de son baptême
et l'entoura de son souffle tout puissant.

5. Vint la nuit obscure qui enveloppa la terre
et puis l'aube en feu du soleil du matin
à nouveau l'Esprit toucha la terre ailes déployées
apportant vie par le feu et par le vent.

2. Viele Menschen sahen in ihren Träumen Leid und Licht,
die der Geist erhellte in der Dunkelheit.
Wüsten wurden Gärten, Menschen fanden neues Glück,
durch die Zeiten setzt sie ihre Reise fort.

3. Wie ein leises Flüstern in der Nacht, berührt von Zärtlichkeit,
nahm Maria ihren Sohn in sich auf;
als ein Kind des Friedens, Gottes stete Gegenwart,
schließt das Lied des Geistes in ihr Herz sie ein.

© 1985 Common Cup Company, Canada. German, Sabine Udodesku-Noll. French, Robert Faerber.

THESE ARE THE WOMEN

Carole Etzler: USA

These are the wo-men who through-out the de-cades have led us and helped us to know. Where we have come from and where we are go-ing, the wo-men who've helped us to grow. Stand-ing be-fore us, mak-ing us strong. Lend-ing their wis - dom to help us a-long, shar-ing a vi - sion, shar-ing a dream, touch-ing our thoughts, touch-ing our lives like a deep flow-ing stream.

© Carole Etzler, PO Box 15307, Atlanta, AN, 30333, USA.

WHO IS MY MOTHER?

Shirley Murray

Ian Render: Aotearoa/New Zealand

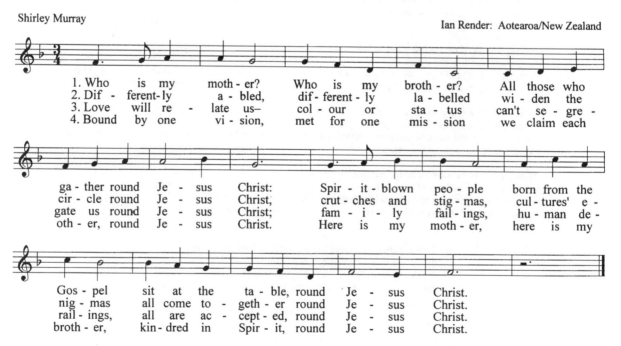

1. Who is my moth - er? Who is my broth - er? All those who ga - ther round Je - sus Christ: Spir - it - blown peo - ple born from the Gos - pel sit at the ta - ble, round Je - sus Christ.
2. Dif - ferent-ly a - bled, dif - ferent - ly la - belled wi - den the cir - cle round Je - sus Christ, crut - ches and stig - mas, cul - tures' e - nig - mas all come to - geth - er round Je - sus Christ.
3. Love will re - late us— col - our or sta - tus can't se - gre - gate us round Je - sus Christ; fam - i - ly fail - ings, hu - man de - rail - ings, all are ac - cept - ed, round Je - sus Christ.
4. Bound by one vi - sion, met for one mis - sion we claim each oth - er, round Je - sus Christ. Here is my moth - er, here is my broth - er, kin - dred in Spir - it, round Je - sus Christ.

Melody BRONWEN, © Ian Render. English, © Shirley Murray.

TUA PALAVRA NA VIDA

Simei Monteiro: Brazil

Tu - a Pa - la - vra na vi - da   é fon - te que ja - mais se - ca,
Your word in our lives, e - ter - nal, it is a clear foun - tain flow - ing;

á - gua que a - ni - ma e res - tau - ra to - dos que a quei - ram be - ber.
wa - ter that gives strength and cou - rage to all who draw near and drink.

2. Tua Palavra na vida é qual semente que brota;
torna-se bom alimento, pão que não há de faltar.

3. Tua Palavra na vida é espelho que bem reflete,
onde nos vemos, sinceros, como a imagem de Deus.

4. Tua Palavra na vida é espada tão penetrante
que revelando as verdades vai renovando o viver.

5. Tua Palavra na vida é luz que os passos clareia,
para que ao fim no horizonte se veja o Reino de Deus.

© 1989 do Instituto Anglicano de Estudos Teológicos, Rua Borges Lagoa,
172-CEP 04038, São Paulo SP, Brazil.

2. Your word in our lives, eternal,
seed of the Kingdom that's growing;
it becomes bread for our tables,
food for the feast without end.

3. Your word in our lives, eternal,
becomes the mirror where we see
the true reflection of ourselves:
children and image of God.

4. Your word in our lives, eternal,
it is a sharp two-edged sword;
dividing our lies from your truth,
it's bringing new life to all.

5. Your word in our lives, eternal,
is light that shines on the long road
that leads us to the horizon
and the bright Kingdom of God.

Words Sonya Ingwersen © 1990 WCC

SOURCES

ILLUSTRATIONS

4: WCC - Salgado Junior

6: WCC - J. Liebenberg

7: WCC - Peter Williams

9: WCC - Peter Williams

12: WCC - Peter Williams

14: WCC - Peter Williams

16: WCC - Peter Williams

18: WCC - Salgado Junior

22: WCC - Peter Williams

26: WCC - Peter Williams

30: WCC - Peter Williams

32: UNICEF - Roger Lemoyne

34: WCC - John Taylor

41: "The Crucifixion" - painting by Perugino - Religious News Service Photo - Radio City Station - New York - USA

43: WCC - Peter Williams

53: WCC - Peter Williams

60: "The three Marys" - Panel, Troyes - France - © Sonia Halliday & Laura Lushington

62: WCC - Michael Dominguez

72: Icon of St. Elizabeth WCC - Peter Williams

76: WCC - Peter Williams

82: WCC - Peter Williams

84: Marie Arnaud Snakkers

100: WCC - Peter Williams

107: WCC - Don Edkins

TEXTS

We wish to thank all those who have granted permission for the use of texts in this book. We have made every effort to trace and identify them correctly and, where necessary, to secure permission to reprint. If we have erred in any way in the acknowledgments, or have unwittingly infringed any copyright, we apologize sincerely.

WOMB SPIRIT

First printed in *Spirit Mourn, Spirit Dance,* published by the United Church of Canada, Etobicoke, Ontario, Canada, August 1998. Used with permission of the author.

WOMAN SONG

"I Come from the Earth", in *What Do We Mean When We Say Sacred?*, ed. Edna J. Orteza, Geneva, WCC, 1998.

"I Come from the Land of Spirits", from Chung Hyun-Kyung's presentation on the theme of the WCC's seventh assembly, Canberra 1991, in *Signs of the Spirit*, ed. Michael Kinnamon, Geneva, WCC, 1991, pp.39-40.

"Quiet Thoughts", in *Women in a Changing World*, WCC, Dec. 1991.

"Who Am I?", in *What Do We Mean When We Say Sacred?*, ed. Edna J. Orteza, Geneva, WCC, 1998.

"Who Am I?", in *Sustainable Development or Malignant Growth?*, ed. 'Atu Emberson-Bain, Suva, Fiji, Marama Publications, 1994.

"I Am a Process", in *What Do We Mean When We Say Sacred?*, ed. Edna J. Orteza, Geneva, WCC, 1998.

"Tribeswoman", in *Igorota*, vol. 5, no. 2, 1991.

"Today Is My Turn to Eat", in *Decade Link*, March 1995.

"He Is the Man", in *What Do We Mean When We Say Sacred?*, ed. Edna J. Orteza, Geneva, WCC, 1998.

"Working Mother", in *Sustainable Development or Malignant Growth?*, ed. 'Atu Emberson-Bain, Suva, Fiji, Marana Publications, 1994.

"Don't Call Me a Stranger", in *World Mission Magazine*, Philippines, vol. 7, no. 3.

"Dowry Deaths", in *In God's Image*, Sept. 1989.

"I Wore the Silken Gown of the Empress", in *Kamalayan: Feminist Writings in the Philippines*, ed. Penny S. Azarcon, Pilipina, 1987.

"i never was a maiden", in *Indigenous Women*, a publication of the Indigenous Women's Network, vol. 1, no. 4.

"I No Longer Spoke of Freedom", in *ACW Newsletter*, April-May-June 1998, Asian Church Women's Conference, Philippines.

"Let Us Choose Life", in *Women in a Changing World*, WCC, Dec. 1991.

"A Woman's Hands", used with permission of the author.

"My Cross", in *Dare to Dream: A Prayer and Worship Anthology from around the World*, ed. Geoffrey Duncan, London, Fount, 1995.

WOMAN, WHY ARE YOU WEEPING?

"Woman, Why Are You Weeping? ", inspired by the biblical reflections during the European Conference on Violence against Women, used with the permission of the author.

"My Child", in *Women and World Religions: Asia-Pacific Women's Studies Journal*, no. 5, 1995, ed. Sr Mary John Mananzan, Manila, Philippines, Institute of Women's Studies and St Scholastica's College.

"Images of Rio", in *Five Loaves and Two Fishes*, ed. Edna J. Orteza, Geneva, WCC, 1998.

"Migrant", in *Asian Journal*, no. 12.

"Pain", in *Dare to Dream*.

"Woman without a Name": this poem refers to Judges 19; used with the permission of the author, c/o Iona Community, Glasgow, Scotland.

"Where Do We Go?", in *In God's Image*, Dec. 1989.

"Give Me Back My Wings", in INSAKA: *Renewing Partnership for Women and Men*, London, Council for World Mission, 1996.

"Uncover the Word", in *Five Loaves and Two Fishes*, ed. Edna J. Orteza, Geneva, WCC, 1998.

"Powerless?", in *In God's Image*, Oct. 1985,

"Rolling Water", written during the Women under Racism global gathering, Port of Spain, Trinidad and Tobago, 1992, published in *Decade Link*, May 1995.

WOMEN, WHY ARE WE STILL WEEPING?

"Women, Why Are We Still Weeping?", used with permission of the author.

"What Does It Mean?", in *Decade Link*, March 1994.

"Remembering the Struggle and Grief of Indigenous Women's Lives", National Commission on Women and Men, Uniting Church in Australia, Sydney.

"O, Women of Asia", in *In God's Image*, Nov. 1983.

"Women of Zambia", in the Decade video *Stand Together with Women*.

"A Decade Lament", used with permission.

"How Can We Sing a New Song?", in *Dare to Dream*.

THE JUSTICE OF WOMEN'S LIBERATION

"The Justice of Women's Liberation", extract from a 19th-century Tamil poet who stood for the cause of social and political freedom as well as the liberation of women in India.

"Veronica", quoted in *A Procession of Prayers*, ed. John Carden, Geneva, WCC, 1998, pp.229-30.

"Rencontre", *Decade Link*, 1994.

"Women and Men Are Partners", in "The Theological Basis of the Decade", *The Ecumenical Review*, vol. 46, no. 2, April 1994, pp.145-46.

"Three Poems", in *Broken Buds*, Mapusa, Goa, The Other India Press, 1994.

"I Am a Woman", in *Our Strength Is Our Hope*, Geneva, WCC, 1996.

"House Maid", translated by Mohiuddin Ahmed, published by Namijan Aftabi Foundation, Jaipurhat, Bangladesh.

"Waking Up from Slumber", in "The Decade: A Man's View", *The Ecumenical Review*, vol. 46, no. 2, April 1994, pp.192-93.

THE GOSPEL ACCORDING TO YOU

"The Gospel According to You", in *In God's Image*, winter 1994.

"Christ Comes to Us Women Today!", used with the permission of the author.

"The Story of Joanna", in *Miriam, Mary and Me*, Toronto, Northstone Publications, 1996, used with permission of the author.

"A Tribute to Rizpah: A Spirituality of Resistance and Transformation", used with the permission of the author.

"The Life of St Nina", in *The St Nina Quarterly*, vol. 1, no. 1, 1997

"St Brigit", in *The St Nina Quarterly*, vol. 1, no. 4, fall 1997.

"Icon Painting as Devotion and Discipline", in *The St Nina Quarterly*, vol. 1, no. 4, fall 1997.

"Surprised by Joy", in *Women on Fire*, ed. Lorna Kalaw-Tirol, Pasig City, Philippines, Anvil Publishing, 1997.

"Setting Our Faces to the New Jerusalem", excerpted from a longer sermon based on Luke 9:51-62, used with permission.

THE SONG OF PEACE

"The Song of Peace", found on an old American calendar.

"The Story of Women", in *Groundswell*, winter 1993, and Decade Link, July 1993.

"Women Make Things Grow", by one of the Palestinian peace negotiators, quoted in *MECC Perspectives*, Middle East Council of Churches, nos 9-10, 1991.

"The Sharing", in *Common Concern*, no. 82, June 1994, and *Decade Link*, June 1994.

"Each Bird", excerpt from "Village of Hope: By the River of Babylon", in *Sustainable Development or Malignant Growth*.

"Regaining the 'We-ness'", in *What Do We Mean When We Say Sacred?*, ed. Edna J. Orteza, Geneva, WCC, 1998.

"From the Dawn of Time", Uniting Church in Australia, Sydney, NSW.

"Throwing a Stone in a Calm Lake", in *Dare to Dream*.

"We Are Going Home to Many Who Cannot Read", in *Seeing Christ in Others*, ed. Geoffrey Duncan, Norwich, UK, Canterbury Press, 1998.

"Jesus Heard the Cries...", in *No Longer a Secret*, Geneva, WCC, 1994.

"Affirming Community", in *Women in a Changing World*, Dec. 1991.

"Rethinking the Concept of Partnership", in *"Women's Journey with and within the SCMs and WSCF": Towards a Women's History in the World Student Christian Federation*, WSCF, 1995.

"Making Solidarity Real", in *Women in a Changing World*, Dec. 1991.

"A New Way of Being", in *Women in a Changing World*, Dec. 1991.

MAGDALENE DANCING IN CRIMSON

"Magdalene Dancing in Crimson", in *Five Loaves and Two Fishes*, ed. Edna Orteza, Geneva, WCC, 1998.

"The Table of Life", in *Five Loaves and Two Fishes*, ed. Edna Orteza, Geneva, WCC, 1998.

"The Web of Life", in *Dare to Dream*.

"Prayers", from I *Will Pour Out My Spirit*, WCC, 1993.

"Mary Maiden Mother", in *In God's Image*, Sept. 1989.

"Litany of Mary of Nazareth", in *In God's Image*, summer 1991.

"Earth Credo", used with permission.

"Mayan Prayer", from the *Popul Vuh*, Mayan book of the Dawn of Life.

"A Prayer for Mother Earth", used with permission.

"Oración por la Mujer", used with permission; part of this prayer, inspired by Francis of Assisi, was published in *Puebla, la hora de María, la hora de la Mujer*, Buenos Aires, 1980.

"Prayer of Thanksgiving on the Occasion of the Year of Indigenous Peoples", used with permission.

"A Prayer from Slovakia", written for this book by the first woman pastor in the Slovak Republic, now 76 years old, who suffered persecution and imprisonment in communist times; her poem has been twice translated – from Slovak to German [by Daniela Horinkova] and then to English.

"Blessings", in "The Spirit of Reimagining: Setting the Stage", *Church and Society*, May/June 1994, published by the Presbyterian Church USA.